FOOD FOR THE JOURNEY

FOOD FOR THE JOURNEY

A Life in Travel

ELIZABETH J. HAYNES

Thistledown Press

Thistledown Press Ltd.
Unit 222, 220 20th Street W
Saskatoon, SK S7M 0W9
www.thistledownpress.com

Names: Haynes, Elizabeth, 1959- author
Identifiers: Canadiana (print) 2025010234X | Canadiana (ebook) 20250102374 | ISBN 9781771872690 (softcover) | ISBN 9781771872720 (EPUB)
Subjects: LCSH: Haynes, Elizabeth, 1959-—Travel. | LCSH: Food tourism. | LCGFT: Travel writing.
Classification: LCC G465 .H39 2025 | DDC 910.4—dc23

Edited by Susan Musgrave
Cover images by DaisyArt (pomegranates), Renata (eggplants)
Cover and book design by Jennifer Lum
Printed and bound in Canada

Thistledown Press gratefully acknowledges the financial assistance of The Canada Council for the Arts, SK Arts, and the Government of Canada for its publishing program.

sk arts

Canada Council for the Arts | Conseil des arts du Canada

Saskatchewan

Funded by the Government of Canada | Financé par le gouvernement du Canada | Canada

For my family

CONTENTS

DESAYUNO

(breakfast)

FOOD FOR THE JOURNEY

I HAVE INHERITED a black-and-white photograph, taken when my father worked for the British Colonial Office in Nigeria. A proper sahib, he sits, hands folded, in the middle of a wooden settee. He is flanked by four Nigerian men. Behind are four boys, mission boys perhaps, in starched white shirts and black bow ties. My father looks into the camera, eyes burning with fear or responsibility. On the back someone has written "W. S. Haynes in Nigeria, fisheries project, 1950s."

Is this recorder on? Okay, this story takes place in northern Nigeria in West Africa. At that time I was living in the Plateau province just south of Panyam at a place called Barakin Ladi . . . We were fish farming and I had to go down to the Benue and tributaries of the Benue to obtain tilapia, which is a perch we used to stock the fish farm. There were tsetse fly zones and we were in a fly-free area and every so often you had to go through a checkpoint. All the vehicles were sprayed with DDT to stop the spread of the fly, which transmitted trypanosomiasis, or African sleeping sickness. It was common throughout all West Africa, and the African people were terrified of sleeping sickness and the fly. [Why, I ask.] *Because sleeping sickness is fatal. We had to go down to oxbow cut-offs and ponds to get our tilapia . . . and when we were going down off the Plateau province down off the escarpment into the jungle— Can you shut that thing off for a minute?*

I am researching Nigeria. Reading about gross national product and geography, imports and exports. Reminds me of social studies class, watching films of dancing women and drumming men, reading books with titles like *The Land and People of . . .* Though I take diligent notes, this does not seem to be what I'm looking for.

In my atlas, Nigeria is only two inches square. So I'll have to invent the dryness of plateau, savannah, the descent into fecundity, river and jungle. Did the Saharan harmattan blow there, filled with dust, like flour, fire? Have to invent, too, this white boy from the prairies: Edmonton, Alberta, Canada. Used to different dust, prairie topsoil, riding behind the tractor at Uncle Wesley's farm at Irma. Used to coulees, lakes, mountains. Dry hot and minus forty cold. How exactly did he, a colonial working for the British Colonial Office, fit in?

Okay, you can turn it back on. We came off the plateau and down into the oxbow cut-offs and ponds and we'd got most of our tilapia for taking back to the fish farm at Panyam when we came upon a village. The people were dead or dying from trypanosomiasis. It was a fly-infected area. In fact, only two or three men would come into the village with me. [Were they Nigerian men?] *Yeah, most of the Nigerian men that were with me wouldn't come because they were all terrified of the tsetse fly.* [Well, weren't you afraid of it too?] *I was kind of young and stupid. But there was nothing anyone could do because the people were dead, lying on the side of the road, in their huts, or in front of their houses. A few of the stronger ones were still alive but I would assume that everyone in the matter of another week would be dead. I notified the assistant district officer but I didn't think anybody could save those people. They were so weak that they couldn't drink or find food for themselves and certainly not cook for themselves. I heard later that the few survivors were evacuated. There was a mass burial and all of the area was completely torched.* [Why?] *Because some of the people had been lying in the heat, in the jungle, dead for about a week . . . The vultures were having a heyday and feeding on the bodies. But it was a very grim memory for me.* [So you were about twenty-five or so?] *No, I was twenty-two, I guess.* [Tell me about that assistant you used to have.] *Jumi* [Who was he?] *A Muslim from Bauchi.* [He wouldn't talk to some of your Christian workers or something?] *Oh yeah, he was a good guy though.* [He was your cook?] *Cook, yeah, everything.*

First time I've listened since I made this tape. Hadn't realized how difficult this was for him. He speaks softly, slowly, trying to conceal from me, his grown daughter. Trying to tell a straightforward story, objectively, like they taught him in medical school. I imagine the fly-laced face of a boy outside a hut. Inside, his mother, dead already. His father's eyes open, close, the stench of flesh, the gathering of vultures. Twenty-two years old. Nothing he or anyone could do.

Sleeping sickness begins with fever, headache, and chills, followed by swelling of the lymph nodes, skin rash, and weakness. The trypanosomes then infect the central nervous system, resulting in uncontrollable sleep, coma, and death.

My father without/before us. I fill in from novels: *Out of Africa*, *The Mottled Lizard*, though these are not the right books. They were before him, from another place, another era. He was in Nigeria half a dozen years before independence, arrived on a freighter, squinting into a bloody sunrise on the Gulf of Guinea. A headful of *Boy's Own* adventure: Stanley, Livingstone, Burton, Speke. Sun poking through leaf, mud huts along a slow river, the beastly heat. What did Jumi cook—roast beef and Yorkshire pudding? Groundnut stew?

On his way back to Edmonton, my father's boat stopped in Rome. He had no money, only his cheque in British West African pounds. Couldn't get it cashed until the embassy stamped it. Three times to the embassy, told to wait, come back tomorrow. Broke, he wandered the city, waiting for the next day when he could eat. The fourth day he threatened to tear the office apart. The cheque was stamped. Hard to imagine my father letting his muscles speak. Though he was not muscled. He'd contracted Weil's disease and malaria. You see, when my six-foot, five-inch father was down to 120 pounds, the British Colonial Service sent him home to die.

He spent that winter bundled in blankets in front of the fire. Trying to get warm.

If I had a calendar here, the pages would blow forward, like in an old movie, SeptOctNovDec. Then he went to med school. Married my mother. Got me. Got his first job, in Williams Lake. Where the cowboys ride at the Williams Lake Stampede.

Is this thing on? Okay, this is in Williams Lake in the 1960s with my good friend and colleague Donald MacLean. We were two young, keen general practitioners. We worked with the public health nurse, a nun, Sister Robert, at Alexis Creek in the Chilcotin. Sister Robert was astute and hard-working. One night we got a call that she was coming in with a sick infant. She had an old van that she brought the kids in with and usually one of the mothers from the reserve would accompany her. She always drove like a bat out of hell but she always got through. She brought the first child in, and the child was very ill with haemophilus influenzae. So we got the child established with a lumbar puncture and all the tests and blood cultures and a cut-down—an insertion of a canula at the ankle in the long saphenous vein—was done as the child was about six months old. We got this established and then Sister went back to the reserve and over a period of three or four days we had an epidemic of haemophilus influenzae meningitis in the Indians around Alexis Creek and the Redstone reserve. And at one time there were eleven children with meningitis, and Donald MacLean and I looked after them. We put a cot on the third floor of the Cariboo Memorial Hospital and we took turns being with them and made sure they were in good shape and that the IVs were going all the time. One child developed a subdural hematoma from the effect of the meningitis and it had to be drained. I sent the child to the neurosurgeon at St. Paul's in Vancouver but all eleven children including the one with cystic hematoma did very well and eventually they all returned to the reserve. Years later, when discussing this, living in the hospital for the greater part of a month, this was foremost in Donald MacLean's memory. We were talking about looking after those children and the days now of Hib vaccine, that's a vaccine for haemophilus infections. With the death rate from meningitis, I think it's a credit to the nursing staff in this small country hospital that not one child died. Okay. [Don't you want to say some more?] *No. How do you turn this thing off?*

I have a colour photo from the Christmas I made this recording. My father is sitting in his green reclining chair in the living room in Westbank, in the Okanagan, where he and my mother have retired. He is surrounded by wrapping paper. We have been clicking pictures all morning and people are no longer posing. Someone has draped a piece of curly pink ribbon around his neck. It hangs down his chest like a forgotten stethoscope. That sadness in his eyes I remember after a patient died.

I think about what a large thing a family is. I thought I heard a poet say the other day that it gets smaller and smaller until eventually it doesn't exist at all. People say that I am my father's daughter. And I have caught my reflection in shop windows, surprised by the same wrinkled forehead, preoccupied frown. I, too, have been to foreign places. Though my travel has been easy, a pack on my back and money in my pocket. I have seen death from a tourist boat on the Ganges, the smoke from the funeral pyres. Used sign language to get by.

My father worries about dying, though he doesn't tell me that. He has sent me a story to edit, set in Williams Lake, about Joe from the Sugar Cane reserve who won a million in the Irish Sweepstakes. Joe didn't take his meds or go for the surgery my father arranged in Vancouver. Died. My dad still thinks it's his fault. His former nurse died recently, cancer—he wished he'd known. And he's had a stroke, disguised it as a "minor vascular episode," thinking we wouldn't know what that meant. That we wouldn't worry.

Last time I was home, I found him Sunday morning in the recliner with the dog on his lap, staring out the front window at the deserted cul-de-sac. He didn't tell me that he couldn't sleep because of his arthritis. Just put on a smile, pulled himself out of the chair, gave me the highway report, advised about my route home. In the kitchen, I watched his big, gnarled hands holding the knife that sliced cleanly through ham and bread and cheese and the fire-red peaches. Food for the journey.

BACK TO THE GARDEN

THE GROUNDS OF THE Mayan palace complex are lush and expansive; the ocean strolling distance away. The sun flames out in spectacular fashion. There is yoga in the Ramada, beach volleyball, ping pong, and golf. Happy hour starts early and slides into happy half day. "The compound," as my dad calls it, is isolated at the end of a long road. Puerto Vallarta, with its art galleries and museums, is a half-hour taxi ride away.

My octogenarian parents are prairie people. They don't golf. They don't swim much. They haven't been to the ocean in years.

I am here because they wanted to escape winter. Traded in their rural time-share for this fancy one. When I arrived, dad told me mom got lost in the huge dining room one breakfast. She's always been directionally challenged, perhaps as a result of her Saskatchewan childhood, where everything was always in plain sight.

Mom is eager to show me the flora and fauna. We stroll the grounds at dusk, stopping beside a tea-coloured pond. Cormorants and herons hide in the shadows. The tangerine sun slides into the water. She points to a shorebird, his long beak bobbing as he siphons up dinner.

"Do you remember the name of that one, dear?"

"I think you're confusing me with another daughter," I joke. Though my three sisters and I were given detailed information about the plumage and habits of the cedar waxwings, juncos, and yellow-bellied sapsuckers that perched on the feeder outside our dining room window in Kamloops, I was terrible at remembering their names. According to my mother, even starlings are darlings. She has never met a bird she doesn't like.

On the way back to our suite, she recites the names of flowers and bushes, still hoping to educate her eldest: fishbone cactus, Mexican marigold. Mom has never met a flower she doesn't like either, even weedy volunteers that spread through prairie like fire through fescue. Sadly, I am also bad on flowers.

Growing up in Biggar, Saskatchewan, in the 1930s, my mom, Jessie, learned to garden from her Scottish mother, my grandmother Jean. Grandma grew radishes, lettuce, and peas, crab apples and currants. When I was a child, from the muddy days of early spring through leaf-crunching fall, my mom could be found outside, on her knees, a battered ice cream bucket containing her trowel, shears, and spade by her side. She planted her rock garden, pruned the rhodos, weeded the carrots, and prepared her gardens for winter. Mom planted purple-red Italian tomatoes that flourished in the long, sunny summers. She grew peas, beans, potatoes. Giant zucchini kept us supplied with green bread. She gave us our own section of the garden to weed and water, so we'd grow green thumbs too.

Mom and I are heading to the Puerto Vallarta botanical gardens outside of town. Walking is difficult for Dad so he's decided to stay at the "compound." Mom is excited to see the gardens, despite an unpredictable ankle that makes walking on uneven surfaces tricky. We take a cab and alight in the centre of town. I walk behind my small mother to the bus stop to make sure she doesn't get distracted by some natural wonder and stumble. When we were kids, all my sisters and I had to do to distract her from, say, the fact that we had housework or dishes to do was ask her to identify a bird. Or to help us find mariposa lilies and yellow johnny-jump-ups in the sage-covered hills behind our house.

The bus to the gardens winds past emerald cliffs, clattering around bends to reveal glimpses of the ocean below. How beautiful this place must have been when it was just a fishing village, before tourists and time-shares. We get off at the top of a hill, cross the highway, and walk down to the gardens, where we lunch. The resident macaw perches on the railing beside us, waiting for his close-up perhaps. We view the orchid collection, admiring one that looks like our favourite childhood lady's slipper, then hike the path that meanders past other lovelies that Mom identifies as bromeliads, sedums, and agave. The footing is tricky, but Mom wants to walk all the trails and insists on descending right to the stream. We pick our way along until blocked by boulders.

"It's getting rough, Mom, and these rocks look slippery and hard to get around. I think we should turn back."

"Oh, let's just go a little further."

"I don't want you to fall. If you hurt yourself, Dad will kill me."

"Come on," she urges. She grabs my hand, like I'm her best childhood friend, Didi, and they're searching the coulees for crocuses. "Let's just see what's around that next bend."

As a child, Mom had the freedom to explore wherever she wanted: in the town, the surrounding coulees, the rail yard where her Scottish dad worked as a hostler's helper, her uncle's farm. A freedom she extended to her daughters, handing us lunches and a thermos full of water as she sent us up into the hills to explore. She kept dead birds she had found in baggies in the freezer, to later give to her friend Anna, a fellow naturalist and amateur taxidermist. Mom grew herbs in cups in our cluttered kitchen beside glasses with toothpick-impaled avocado pits in water and the drying wishbones of holiday birds.

When she was a bairn and there were chores to do, she ran away. When my grandma tried to show her how to can preserves or make a pie crust, she'd slip out the back door. I imagine Mom and Didi, armed with empty syrup pails for Saskatoon berries, roaming far and wide, missing dinner. I picture them on their backs in my great-uncle's wheat field, counting cloud animals and red-tailed hawks in that big sky.

On our second-last day at the compound, we take a tour with my parents' favourite socialist tour guide, Miguel, who had previously escorted them around a mining town and a coffee plantation. A trip which, to their delight, included a detailed labour history. Our destination: a distant Huichol village. It will be a long bus ride, I warn my parents, six hours on bad roads, I say, but fascinated by the Huichol yarn and bead art they've seen in town, they are determined to go. We eventually find ourselves in a tiny cluster of huts on the top of a hill, overlooking a wide valley. Miguel has only recently started bringing tourists here and cautions us to be respectful. Yes, the villagers may be poor, but they are strong people with an ancient spiritual tradition which includes honouring the peyote. This sacred plant is featured in their art, yarn paintings, and bead-encrusted gourds. Which we should buy, Miguel says. One or more pieces per family, he suggests. As Dad chats with the teenage sellers in Spanglish, selecting paintings for my sisters, Mom and I wander to the edge of a cliff. She pulls out her binoculars and we watch the raptors riding up and down the thermals.

My mother told me this story. In 1953, she left Carrot River, where she had adjudicated a drama festival, on a train bound for Nipawin, where she was living and teaching. It was blizzarding. The track hadn't been cleared of snow and the train was eventually forced to stop. The conductor told my mother and the four other people on board to get off and walk to the tracks that intersected their line and had been cleared. One of the five was a pregnant woman. The wind whirled snow around them. Visibility dropped. The little group walked through knee-high drifts as the snow got heavier and the temperature fell. Finally, someone thought he saw a distant farmhouse and they left the safety of the tracks, wading through waist-deep snow toward the farmhouse, which I imagine kept disappearing and reappearing, house then mirage, house, mirage. House. The farmer and his wife welcomed the exhausted band, let them warm up, fed them, and drove them to the railway station.

I suspect that they could have easily been lost in that blizzard, could have succumbed to the cold, died of hypothermia. But my mother related this story with a smile on her face. They were almost lost, yes. It was cold. It was difficult. But she met some wonderful people—her fellow travellers, the farmhouse couple who were so kind and generous. And wasn't it all such a great adventure!

I've always preferred living in big sky places. In my twenties, I spent two winters in Terrace, British Columbia, where the fog and winter inversions, the looming mountains, withered my spirit, became heavy. A burden.

My mother's maiden name is Porter, which means a carrier of burdens. But I think my mother, and her mother before her, carried their burdens lightly. My Grandma Jean's loss of her first husband and three brothers in World War I. My mom's illnesses and battles.

Ten years after that Mexico trip, my parents live in a seniors' "resort." Chosen for its location beside a nature trail and creek and because there are raised plots where they can plant a garden. My mom can enjoy nature, pushing her walker down the path, her chest still tender from recent surgery, searching for the great horned owl she has once seen; the golden eyes she hopes to see; the first yellow balsam roots of spring.

My mom taught me to look at what was below me: to search a coulee bank for the first spring flowers, to look up for the red-winged blackbird flitting along the bulrushes, the hawk riding air.

In early retirement, my mother took up *kadō*, the Japanese way of the flowers. The drained and covered hot tub in their home, initially installed to ease arthritic joints, became the ikebana table. Mom collected interesting looking twigs and branches. Cut Oregon grape and brought in flowers: a single iris, a tulip, a sunflower from her garden. She started an *ikebana* club, hired a local teacher, studied with a sensei who came from Japan to teach classes. Spent hours collecting and arranging. Gave up the practice only when her arthritic fingers refused to co-operate any more, to snip and bend, to fashion the scalene triangle symbolizing heaven, human, earth. She gave up quietly. Without a fuss. She still had her garden.

SOULS OF THE ANCESTORS: WALKING AROUND TORAJALAND

ON A WALL IN THE RANTEPAO, Tana Toraja tourist office is a large whiteboard. On the board are pencilled dates and locations for this week's funerals and house-blessing ceremonies. On the right are numbers representing the number of pigs and buffalo to be slaughtered at each one. My sister Jocelyn and I have hitched a ride to this inland city on the Indonesian island of Sulawesi, part of our eight-month backpacking trip through Asia. We were intrigued by stories we heard about this remote part of Indonesia from other backpackers. But neither of us has ever been to a funeral. The only person we know who died is our grandpa, and though we were school-aged, our parents felt we were too young to attend. We scribble down information on house-blessings.

The Torajans live in isolation in hilltop villages in the south-central highlands of Sulawesi, hunting and practising their animist religion, Aluk Todolo, worship of the spirit of the ancestors, until the Dutch arrived in 1906. The Dutch subdued the Torajans with bullets, as per usual for conquerors, then marched them down into the valleys. They banned headhunting, fertility ceremonies, and the 7,777 ritual taboos.

They introduced agriculture and Christianity. Today, approximately 60 percent of Torajans practise Christianity, though they spice it heavily with Aluk Todolo.

Walking the streets of Rantepao, people stop Joc and me to ask "Are you Christian?" I remember asking my mom what religion we were for a school form and her response: "Just put down United." So we tell them yes. On Sunday morning, we search in vain for an open restaurant. It seems everyone is at church. Yet I read Torajans spend a great deal of their lives trying to accumulate wealth because in *puya,* the hereafter, they are destined to live in the same conditions that they did on earth. And the more pigs and buffalo slaughtered at your funeral the better, for their souls follow the dead to *puya*. An attractive concept, though I don't believe in an afterlife. When you're gone, you're gone.

In the nearby village of Batutumonga, there is a soul waiting to enter *puya*. It belongs to Mama Siska's grandmother. Her partially embalmed body apparently lies, as it has for two years, in a room at the back of Mama Siska's house. Mama Siska is trying to bring her scattered relatives together for the funeral, trying to make enough money to buy a buffalo to sacrifice. So she has started to take in tourists, Joc and me among them. Lying close together on the wooden platform that is our bed at night, we whisper that we hope grandma's soul isn't restless, hasn't taken to wandering at night. We keep a flashlight close by. In the day, we avoid the back of the house, which smells just fine.

Little Siska, Mama's daughter, skips in front of Jocelyn and me, along the muddy paths through misty green fields of terraced rice. She is taking us to see a *rante*—a field with large stones, monuments to the ancestors. As we arrive at this funeral site, the rain begins, lightly at first then more insistent. I imagine men building these *tongkonan*, upside-down boathouses, to contain the grieving relatives, carefully carving and painting on them in red, white, yellow, and black, the traditional geometric designs. The Torajans sailed to Sulawesi seven thousand years ago from Kampuchea in the north. They heaved their boats ashore, aligned them north, and then turned them upside down to make shelters. New *tongkonan* are still built facing north.

Walking the path back to Mama Siska's homestay, little Siska sings a Torajan version of "Michael Row the Boat Ashore." We sing along in English, causing her to giggle and grow suddenly shy.

We decide to go the village of Bori to see a house-blessing ceremony. Our guide, Johannes, provided by the tourist office, leads Joc and me through the crowds to a wooden platform thronged with smoking, drinking men and abandons us. "Where is he going?" I whisper to Joc, and she shrugs. A passing woman hands us glasses of *tuak* (palm wine) and a plate of *pa'piong*, meat and vegetables cooked with coconut and pig's blood in bamboo tubes. Johannes reappears, telling us to follow him, quickly, it is time for the pig kill. Suddenly I am not so keen to see a pig die. We trail him to an open area where girls in beaded skirts dance to the fierce beating of drums. We are soon surrounded by laughing men and women and squealing children and pigs, the latter imprisoned in brightly decorated bamboo cages. A pig is freed, a man catches him, unsheathes a knife, and slits the animal's throat. Little boys with bamboo tubes swoop in to catch the flowing blood. So much blood. Joc and I look at each other as if to say this will be our first and only attendance at an animal sacrifice.

The next day in Lemo, we stare up at rows of *tau-tau*, wide-eyed wooden effigies of the dead crowding each other in the cliff niches high above us. Wearing clothes that are changed yearly by the deceased's relatives, these representations of the spirit watch over the cliff graves of their wealthy masters. I ponder the ingenuity of the Torajans. They began burying their dead in cliff and hanging graves to stop outsiders from stealing the gold and jewels interred with the bodies in the ground. And how lovely that they buried babies in trees to allow the babies' souls to continue to grow with the branches.

On our last day in Tana Toraja, we decide to take a short hike from Sangalla to Suaya. Starting out, we notice a young man following us. I look back nervously, thinking maybe he wants money, and the man, taking this as an invitation, runs to join us. His name is Tony. He is a teacher who wants to practise his English. He has no ulterior motive but to walk and talk with us and I feel ashamed of my unkind thoughts. At Suaya, we walk around the heavy stone coffins topped with skulls and bones, arranged artfully I think, for tourists.

As we follow Tony back across the sun-drenched fields, I ponder death as a beginning not an end, a portal to a new life, something that informs future lives. We pass men carrying fighting cocks in bamboo cages and women laden with baskets of produce. They call "*Selamat sore*," good afternoon. Children point at us and cry "*Belanda*," which Tony tells us means Dutchwomen. In Sangalla, we search for a *bemo* to take us back to Rantepao but they are all crowded with market people and their baskets, so we walk the seven kilometres to the main road. Rain drums gently on our umbrellas. A man and buffalo plow a field below us. Above, gossamer mist, like spirits, hovering.

MEMBER OF A WEDDING: A SHORT SOUTHERN SOJOURN

I AM IN JOCELYN'S GREEN MONTE CARLO, windows down, driving from the airport to her house in Raleigh. The midnight air is steamy, there's the smell of wet earth and moulding leaves. Kudzu vines and Spanish moss drape the trees lining this country road. Joc and I pass an old black man driving a rusted pickup, a kudzu-covered shack, a primitive Baptist church. The sky is drowning in stars, the road deserted.

I am the first to arrive for Joc's wedding. My kind, funny little sister is marrying Steve, the tall, red-headed son of a Swedish father and German Mennonite mother, Connecticut- and North Carolina–raised. Steve's family is devout Methodist. Our family is lapsed United. The wedding will take place in a nineteenth-century Moravian church in Winston-Salem, near Kernersville, where his family lives. The minister, a family friend, is Presbyterian/Quaker, a former Freedom Rider and political activist. Steve's sister will be reading from the biblical Song of Solomon. My sister Leslie will read from *The Prophet*. I have a few days with Joc to recreate the closeness we had in the eight-month backpacking trip to Asia we took a few years ago. I want to talk about our old adventures. Her new adventure. But first we must eat.

"Dinner in a diner, nothing could be finer
Than to have your ham and eggs in Carolina."

In Baxley's to be exact, because I asked to go out for an authentic Southern breakfast, like the ones I had when visiting my family in Alabama the 1980s. We order pancakes, bacon, eggs, grits (kind of like cream of wheat with butter and salt), and biscuits. Though I draw the line at gravy.

Joc and I talk. Okay, I talk: about how everything is so green and lush here, how friendly people seem. The smell of bacon drifts from the kitchen, a fan pushes the lazy air around.

"I love coming to a new place, how the senses are sharpened, and everything seems new. That's why I love travelling."

Joc smiles, nods. She's a great listener, my little sis.

"You're awfully quiet."

"Well, you seem to need to talk."

Maybe she doesn't want to burst my bubble about the reality of life in North Carolina—the conservative politics, the high illiteracy rate, the gap between rich and poor. Or is just preoccupied with wedding plans.

It's Friday—a work day for Joc and Steve. I climb into the Monte Carlo and, with all four windows down, head down the Beltline to the North Carolina Museum of Art. I unpeel the back of my sweaty legs from the vinyl seat and go inside. Ah, the joys of air conditioning.

I wander through rooms filled with medieval and renaissance Christs to the contemporary section. Gaze at an Andrew Wyeth painting of a young boy, fingers outstretched, running down a hill. It is titled *Winter, 1946*. The same year Carson McCullers published *The Member of the Wedding*, about Frankie, a twelve-year-old girl wandering around her

Southern town rebelling against the strictures of society and race, waiting for her brother's wedding and dreaming of escape.

Deciding to postpone my return to the sauna outside, I venture downstairs to the museum café. I'm escorted to a table. Sitting, I notice that my sandalled toes are dirty. The Southern ladies, straight out of Carson McCullers's novel, wear crisp linen dresses in pastel shades. Their toes are covered. The waitress brings my sweet tea—in Alabama I learned that "tea" means iced tea and when ordering must be preceded by the adjectives sweet or unsweet. "Can I get you anything else, ma'am?" the young waitress asks me. Ma'am? A ma'am is surely much older than me.

We visit Raleigh's Reader's Corner, a big, high-ceilinged, nook-and-crannied, book-jammed place with yellowed newspaper clippings on the walls: Hemingway in Cuba, a Faulkner memorial. They have a copy of *The Member of the Wedding*, which I peruse. Remember that poor Frankie had hoped to go to Alaska with her brother and his fiancée on their honeymoon, where she would live a big and adventurous life.

At Steve's Ice Cream beneath humming air conditioners, we read the free weekly news mags. We start with the *Triangle Comic Review* ("serving the Raleigh, Durham and Chapel Hill areas"), flip past an ad for Noah's Co-op Grocery (where Elvis was recently sighted), past a cartoon showing Bush I grilling a taxpayer on a backyard barbecue labelled Savings and Loan, then move on to the *Spectator*, featuring ads for a Lebanese bakery, Persian rugs, Birkenstocks, and a feature on the "Best in the Triangle," including Best Vacant Lot (Republican Senator Jesse Helms's mind), and the *Independent*, with its scathing editorial on Nancy Reagan.

Why this hive of counterculture writing in a state known for its conservative, Tobacco Is King mentality? I ask Joc. She reminds me there are three big universities in close proximity: the University of North Carolina at Chapel Hill, North Carolina State, and Duke, not to mention the Research Triangle Park, which boasts the highest density of PhDs in North America.

The rest of the members of the wedding have arrived: my sister Les and her boyfriend from New York, my other sister Mel from Vancouver, Mom and Dad from Kelowna, my aunt from Whitehorse. We are sitting with Joc and Steve's friends and their two dogs on the back deck. Sweetgums and yellow poplars tower above us; the back neighbour's house is barely visible through the tangle of greenery. The air conditioner purrs, a car backfires up the road, a mockingbird calls. We're eating perogies (Aunt Agnes's speciality) and barbecued kubasa (found, after a lengthy search, at the Piggly Wiggly), drinking coolers, talking of who is arriving next, and planning sightseeing junkets. The conversation meanders from Steve studying engineering to engineering in Canada to Kipling penning the Canadian engineering ode to Kipling writing *The Jungle Book* to my father, who has possibly had one too many coolers, standing up and leading us in a rousing rendition of the Boy Scout grand howl: "Ah-kay-la! We will do our best! Dyb-dyb-dyb-dyb, dob-dob-dob-dob."

The big day arrives. I drive Mom and Aunt Agnes to the church to arrange the flowers. The Moravian church is simple but beautiful: wood benches, polished by two and a half centuries of use; whitewashed walls; the only decoration a few pewter candlesticks. Light floods in through high windows. I leave the cool inside for the sauna outside, drive the Monte

Carlo to pick up my nervous father, who insists on both driving back and ignoring my attempts to direct him ("Turn left here, Dad. Yes I'm sure, I just drove this road.")

In the vestry, Mom and the matron of honour, Michele, fuss over Joc's hair. In her simple fitted white dress, my little sister is beautiful, calm and smiling. We take our seats and our father walks her down the aisle. Joc's voice is clear and strong as she takes her vows. At the reception, we eat German potato salad, spanakopita, dolmades, and Swedish meatballs, dance to Les's mixed tape of reggae, folk, blues, and rock, while Steve's Mennonite aunts from Ohio watch, nod, and smile.

Sunday. Joc and Steve have left for a Maritime honeymoon, Mom and Dad are escorting friends through the Blue Ridge Parkway, Les and Mario have left for New York. Mel, Michele, and I have driven the Monte Carlo back to Raleigh. Joc and Steve's friends take us to an Italian place near North Carolina State University for dinner. After stuffing ourselves with handmade calzone, we wander down to the ice cream shop and take our cones to the monument across the street to eat. A guy with a guitar is playing James Taylor. My little sister and her husband are off on a new adventure. I am so very happy for them. Though I feel a bit left behind. Like Frankie.

ALMUERZO

(lunch)

RIDING THROUGH REVOLUTION

IT IS THIRTY-TWO DEGREES and windless. My cycling *compañeros* are nowhere in sight. I'm grinding up the hill to Puerto Boniato in eastern Cuba, trailing laughing kids in red school uniforms and trying like hell to remember the Spanish word for top so I can ask if it is close. My legs strain the pedals of my twenty-one-speed, my granny gear is engaged, I can't go any lower.

My sister Melissa and our guide, Reg, are waiting at the top, apparently sweat-free, talking of *termos*, cold beer trucks where you can fill up your water bottle for three pesos, or twenty cents. Reg is a former Torontonian, a bike and motorcycle racer now married to Leo (Leonor), a Cuban. Mel is raring to go but Reg suggests they wait until I've had a drink. Then they take off, and I cautiously start down several kilometres of switchbacks. Thank God my bike, unlike many of the Chinese Forever one-speeds ridden by the Cubans, has brakes.

My sister is trying to extricate herself from a verbally abusive relationship with a guy I like to call Jerko. She is skittish, hypervigilant, as if someone's going to lecture her for some minor infraction—incorrectly loading the dishwasher, not closing the window properly. If someone speaks to her in Spanish, she immediately calls me over to help her.

Our younger sisters, Jocelyn and Leslie, were the athletes in our family, played basketball, baseball, soccer. We all played tennis because our dad insisted, because he cut off wooden John McEnroe and Rod Laver racket handles so they would fit our small hands, sat patiently with a bucket of balls across the net from us, hitting to our forehand, backhand, lob, coaching us for hours on our serve. Joc had a killer forehand and backhand.

Mel and I just played tennis. In high school, I used to be able to beat her because she had grown so fast and was a bit uncoordinated. In her twenties, she joined a club and could soon beat me handily.

The only good thing Jerko did for Mel was introduce her to cycling. Now, a couple of hundred kilometres daily is a cinch for her. In a day, she can blast through several Gulf Islands, ride to Hope and back. Once when I was visiting we decided to cycle to Galiano Island. We rode from her house in Surrey to the Tsawwassen ferry. On the island we rode to our B and B, me on my heavy, second-hand mountain bike, she on her light, custom-made Marinoni. When we finally reached our destination, I cursed the hilliness of islands. She proposed an evening ride. The next day she convinced me to circumnavigate Galiano in the pouring rain. We found ourselves on a mucky dirt path that billed itself as a road. She kept spinning out on her skinny tires. I had the mountain bike and for once was ahead.

We are staying in Santiago de Cuba, the eastern city Fidel Castro called "rebellious yesterday, hospitable today, heroic always." It is the capital of the province of the same name, which contains 70 percent of Cuba's Sierra Maestra. Fidel and his men, aided by peasants and farmers in the poor and sparsely populated countryside, fought much of the revolution here. I am here to write a story for an outdoor magazine, and to indulge my interest in all things Cuban, a passion I developed after a trip here two years ago. I invited my sister to join me on this trip, thinking she'd never come, that her partner would sabotage it somehow. Miraculously, she came.

Seven weeks of cycling around flat and temperate Havana, where I was studying Spanish and Cuban culture, have not prepared me for the thirty-five-degree heat and rugged terrain of Santiago de Cuba province. My sister has no problem, though she is unaccustomed to the catcalls of the men we pass. Men, singly or in pairs, walking by the side of the road, men watching from benches in parks, carrying machetes or bags of fruit, stop and watch us go by. "*Muchachas bonitas*," one calls (our beauty presumably being readily apparent under helmet, sunglasses, and rivers of sweat). "*Novias*," cries another, opening his arms to potential girlfriends, "*Buenas ciclistas*," and, my favourite, an old man who calls "Hi friend, it's nice." Men throw us kisses, men hiss at us (a popular way to get someone's attention here). A Japanese fellow student at my Havana school, the Instituto Superior de Arte, grew weary of hearing "*China linda*" (beautiful Chinese girl) and "*Me matas*" (you kill me) whenever she passed. I've heard that if a woman goes out and gets no *piropos*, she thinks she must look bad and goes home to fix herself up. But it is all in fun, I think, not mean-spirited, not a throwback to another era, as North Americans tourists might think.

The next day, Reg proposes to take us on a thirty-kilometre cycling tour of the city. "To get you used to the heat and hills," he says.

He means Sandra, the other trip participant, a Nicaragua-born travel agent from Toronto, and me. Sandra doesn't want to do much cycling because of her hair, which is lovely, long, and chestnut brown. It takes hours to comb out, she says, after an afternoon of riding. She does want *sapotes*. She has all the staff at the hotel on the lookout for them. Every day someone arrives with the sweet, pink-orange fruit in a plastic bag. She hadn't eaten *sapotes* since she left Nicaragua. Sandra is pleasant, charming, sweetly demanding. Mel and I have nicknamed her the Princess.

"Great!" says Mel, who loves hills. She does them twice. She barely breaks a sweat on them.

"Oh no," Sandra laughs. "I haven't ridden a bike in twenty years. The last time was in Nicaragua."

Melissa looks distressed at this piece of news.

A few years ago, Mel and I decided to cycle from our parents' house in Westbank to Peachland, B.C., in the middle of a scorching summer day. She stopped once to wait, and asked me what was taking me so long when I finally caught up to her.

I lied, said I'd had to change a flat.

Drought Hill almost finished me off.

At the designated spot in Peachland, she was waiting, along with our dad who had driven down to meet us.

Arriving, I collapsed on the ground, dizzy, my head pounding, my hands shaking the water out of the bottle before I could get it to my mouth.

"Your sister's got sunstroke," Dad accused. "Didn't you stop to check on her?"

"I did. She said she was okay."

"Well she's not," said my doctor father. "Neither of you should be riding in this heat."

Dad drove me back. Mel insisted on cycling. Not sure why I had expected her not to leave me behind.

We head down the hill to town, passing Céspedes Park, where comrades argue the finer points of Communist theory under leafy ceiba trees, and the Poder Popular building where Fidel Castro gave his victory speech that ended the Cuban revolution and the reign of the dictator, Batista, on January 2, 1959. I think about the man in Havana who approached me outside Hemingway's favourite bar, La Bodeguito del Medio.

"Do you like Cuba?" he asked.

"Yes. I love it."

He lowered his voice. "You have a good government in your country?"

"Well, it's Conservative. So no."

"But it's a democracy, yes?"

He didn't wait for an answer. "Here the government is terrible," he said, and went on to tell me about his distrust of politicians. He was the first person I'd met in Cuba who talked to me like this. I told him I'd been to many countries in Latin America and that Cuba was miles ahead of every one of them in education, in health care, in women's rights.

"I don't see any homeless children. I don't see children living in garbage dumps. I don't see children begging."

"You're a Communist," he accused.

"Maybe," I said.

"Try to live here," he muttered darkly. "You would not be one any more."

The Rancho Club, where we are staying, is full of Cubans. Usually, foreigners are not allowed to stay at establishments where you pay in Cuban pesos instead of dollars, but Reg and

Leo have arranged it. The motel consists of a series of modest rooms strung out around a pool and patio/outdoor restaurant and bougainvillea-filled garden. The pool is always full of noisy Cuban kids, the outdoor patio dense with couples drinking beer and rum, salsa blasting from speakers. We have been getting up early and cycling for three or four hours, then having lunch and a swim. A perfect day for me. But forty or sixty kilometres is not nearly enough exercise for my sister.

"Go cycle by yourself," I say.

"What if I get lost?"

"Ask for directions. It's a safe country. The worst that will happen is a couple of marriage proposals."

"I don't know any Spanish."

"Sign language works," I mutter. Yes, a bit jealous of my sister, who is getting all the attention while I do all the planning and talking.

I go for a sullen swim, then get over myself and join her on the patio where we watch the passing parade. A waitress comes around with tickets for a roast suckling pig that is being auctioned off. We decline a ticket but given the possibility of eating meat, a luxury here, many people are buying. A few minutes later the winner is drawn and a shout goes out. The lucky ticket holder is from a table of Cubans. I pass by them not long afterwards. Only the carcass remains. What did I expect? The people, as the Cuban I met outside Hemingway's bar in Havana might say, are hungry.

Sandra invites Mel and me to go to a mass in a Santiago church. Mel doesn't want to go. I tell her I'll just be gone an hour.

"Where the hell were you?" my sister demands when we return to the hotel three hours later.

"It was a full mass, in Latin. The priest was on Cuban time. We had to stay for the whole thing because she wanted to talk to the priest afterward. She figured he might have the inside scoop on where to get the best *sapotes*," I joke.

"I thought something happened to you."

Ah, my sweet, gentle sister. Always worried about everyone else. Everyone but herself.

I fell in love with this country in 1997, on a month-long "friendship" tour where I visited hospitals, schools, and daycares in different parts of the country. I "smuggled in" men's underwear, lipstick, children's clothes for the family of my Cuban-Canadian friend, Mercedes, and became friends with her family: Richard (Ricardo, but he likes to go by his English name), Aida, Juana, and their mom, Caridad.

Prior to the cycling trip, I stayed in the dorm with foreign art students. The *tias* or aunts who looked after us made sure that no unauthorized Cubans entered the dorm, called maintenance when the jury-rigged "hot showers" began shooting sparks, introduced us to the complexities of Colombian soap operas.

I should have been studying in an intermediate class but they only offered beginner and advanced so I was put in advanced. Even though I could only understand about half of what Gisela, our teacher, said at first, the class was interesting. We studied poetry, debated the merits of nuclear power, watched films about slavery and the great Cuban literacy campaign of 1961, where students went to the countryside to teach their *compañeros* to read. Learned about how the whole country celebrates International Women's Day. Our materials were typed with a manual typewriter on the backs of Chinese faxes. Despite the hours of homework I had to do to keep up with my fellow students, I loved the class.

The *autopista* outside Santiago is four lanes of smooth black-top with horse- and ox-drawn carts, and goats and cows grazing by the side of the road, but few cars. Gas is expensive and hard to find here due to the U.S. embargo and lack of Russian help. Yarelis, Reg's twelve-year-old stepdaughter who only learned to ride a bike two weeks ago, leads the final climb to the seventeenth-century Morro Castle, which guards the entrance to Santiago Bay, fourteen kilometres south of the city.

After clambering around on the limestone towers, Yare leads us down the snaking coastal road back toward town. We pass a red-and-white Ford from the 1950s on its side, and a few minutes later, the passengers, unhurt and walking toward town; then old wooden mansions, summer homes of the rich before the revolution, their shutters faded, paint peeling.

Later, we go with Leymi, a relative of Leo's, to Granjita Siboney, where Fidel and his M-26-7 rebels planned the attack on the Moncada barracks. We walk around looking at gruesome pictures of the tortured and murdered men. With a voice full of passion and indignation, Leymi tells us that the men were tortured and killed elsewhere then brought back to Granjita Siboney and made to look as if they were caught in their plotting and killed there. I translate for Mel and we both become quiet, thinking of these young men, the age of Leymi, gunned down for the sake of their beliefs.

One day, we head north then west on the Carretera Central, past a centre for "re-education" and private vegetable farms, which have been allowed in recent years to supplement the ration card and farmers' earnings, with growers giving a percentage of their earnings to the state. Oxen and men pull plows, cattle egrets watch from the furrows. Our destination is the mining town of El Cobre, famous for its shrine to Cuba's patron saint, the black Virgen de la Caridad, and an easy (according to Mel) twenty-kilometre ride from Santiago.

We climb the last kilometres to the basilica on bikes, unlike the thousands of pilgrims who yearly crawl up the winding road to fulfill promises to the Virgin. No one is on their knees today, though we pass people walking or riding ox carts. The road has been widened and the church painted yellow in anticipation of a pope's visit which didn't materialize. The government felt the hills provided too many places for antipapists to hide.

Inside the Salon of Miracles, I stare at dolls, letters, war medals, tiny silver body parts called *milagros*: all offerings to the Virgin. Here Lina Ruz, mother of Fidel and Raúl Castro, offered a gold figure to the Virgin for protection of her young sons. Lina, a servant in the household of Fidel's father, Ángel, would bear him five other children and eventually marry him.

We head back to town, coasting down the Avenida de las Americas, trailing dogs. Reg leads us on a shortcut behind a cement plant, where we pass men carrying flowers for wives and mothers in honour of International Women's Day. I wonder if Jerko ever bought Mel flowers. Maybe, when he was trying to woo her and his controlling tendencies were still hidden.

"Viva Fidel, Viva el 40 Aniversario de la Revolución" proclaim white stones on the hillside. I ride past a schoolyard of shouting kids and a sign that says "Youth with the Lineage of Guerillas," another proclaiming "Yesterday for History, Today for Victory." Revolutionary billboards proliferate on this thirty-kilometre ride to the beaches of Buey Cabón and Caletón

Blanco. Reading them, I think how refreshing it is having billboards featuring not anorexic models but moral slogans, quotations exhorting people to work, to uphold the ideals of the revolution.

Cycling along a truck-laden refinery road, I pass a billboard picturing the working "hands of Che" Guevara. Che's hands were cut off after his murder in Bolivia, where he was captured trying to foment revolution. The sign, ironically, towers over the cranes of the free-trade zone.

Melissa and Reg wait for me at the turnoff to the Mar Verde Road, then race ahead to meet Sandra, Reg's wife Leo, and her Cuban friend Mavis, who have taken a taxi to Buey Cabón beach. The traffic thins to the odd truck pulled by horses with kids on bikes hanging on for the ride. The road shimmers blue in the midday heat as I look out to the scrubby, green foothills of the Sierra Maestra cascading down to the sea.

We are just getting settled on the beach when the police arrive. Since a recent speech of Fidel's, the police are attempting to stamp out prostitution, and Cuban-foreigner relationships are discouraged. Leo, Reg, and Mavis are questioned by the officers. Leo and Reg must produce their marriage licence and Mavis is not allowed to sit with us. I glance over at a group middle-aged Italian guys with their young Cuban girlfriends. I silently applaud when the police come for them, am frustrated when I see they take away the girls, leaving the men to enjoy the beach.

We are sitting, Mel, Eduardo, and I, on metal chairs outside La Rueda bar in Siboney. Eduardo has accompanied us to this town where Leo and Reg have arranged a *casa particular* (private B and B) for us. I'm not exactly sure of Eduardo's relationship to Leo—her small house is always full of friends and relatives. A cousin maybe? Second cousin? Whoever he is, he has taken a fancy to Mel. He is short but handsome, probably a decade younger than my sister. I, as usual, am the translator.

"Is she married?"

"No."

"Does she like Cuban men?"

"Do you like Cuban men, Mel?"

She giggles. "Yes."

"She has beautiful eyes."

Baby harp seal eyes, we call them in the family.

"Your eyes are stunning."

More giggling.

"Would she marry a Cuban man?" Eduardo asks, monologuing on.

"What is he saying?" She is smiling, girlish. I haven't seen her like this for a long time.

"Okay, it appears he's proposing marriage. Says you would have beautiful children together. They would have brown skin and blue eyes. You would raise them yourself in Canada, but they would come frequently to visit their *papi*. You want me to continue translating?"

She nods. I sigh.

"Your sister is very tall," Eduardo begins again.

"Yes."

"She is a model, I think."

"She's a pharmacist."

"Why is she not married?"

"She lives with someone."

"Perhaps she will leave him."

"*Ojalá*," I say. God willing.

"Why?"

"It's a long story."

"He had an affair?'

"Probably. He's a controlling . . ." I don't know the word in English.

"*Pendejo*?" Eduardo asks. Asshole.

"*Pendejo. Exacto.*"

In the dark, after too many mojitos, we weave our way back to our *casa particular*. Eduardo walks close beside my sister. He insists on coming up the back stairs. Says he wants to ask Mel something, alone. I leave them on the patio. Ten minutes later I pop my head outside. He is whispering, presumably Spanish, in her ear. No need for translation, I guess.

"You okay?"

"Yup."

"Is he bothering you?"

"Nope.

"Are you sure?"

"Obviously. I'm a big girl. Go inside. I'll be fine."

At thirteen, Mel grew into her new, tall body so quickly, her limbs stopped obeying; her hips were permanently bruised due to her difficulty negotiating corners. She left cups to dangle precariously on the edge of counters, or set them in the air where she thought the counter was. My parents' friends thought she should be a model. Doc Hebden, her high school science teacher, thought she should be a physicist. She was shy, known as a brain, top of the class in math. Top of the class in everything. Boys were not aware of her existence.

We didn't always get along. In high school we fought. Terrible, hair-pulling, kicking, scratching fights that scared our two younger sisters. Mom said Mel just wanted attention. She said things to provoke me, would threaten to tell Mom about my drinking, my secret pot stash. I teased her mercilessly. One day, she got so upset about something at dinner she overturned her plate, ran outside to our swimming pool, looked at us defiantly through the dining room window, and dove in with all her clothes on.

As a toddler, her speech was hard to understand. Older by two years, I would try to talk for her, interpret her words, and she would scream in frustration, wanting to talk for herself.

In college, we had the same English professor. A Scottish man with long hair, sideburns, round John Lennon glasses, and two outfits, one a green velvet suit, the other a purple velvet suit, which he wore with puffy, long-sleeved white shirts and matching velvet vests (though sometimes he wore the contrasting-coloured vest). He was larger than life, an eccentric intellectual in a B.C. town with too few of them. He introduced me to Lawrence, Koestler, Hemingway, Pynchon. I adored him and spent countless hours on my essays for his class. Mel had him two years later and adored him equally. English had always been my best subject, chemistry hers. I got an A minus. Mel got an A. Yes, she was good in English too.

La Improvisada store in Dos Caminos has nothing in it, though La Invasora in San Luis has a few goods on dusty shelves. A monument to General Moncada states, "My black arms and my Cuban heart have faith in victory." "Each man dies well if he dies while working," proclaims a Dos Caminos billboard.

Riding twenty-five kilometres north on the *autopista*, we turn right on the Dos Caminos Road, passing sugar cane fields and a mill, then swoop down the *autopista* and climb up to Puerto Boniato, and down to Boniato. Here we encounter our first *termos*. Ten a.m. is an absurd time to be drinking beer, but we fill our water bottles anyway, chatting with the young "barman" who requests our addresses, says he wants to write to us in Canada.

The beer is cool, refreshing. Fortified, we ride through the quiet, cobbled streets of El Caney, turn left at the sign to El Escandel then right to a fort. The road to El Escandal, Reg says, turns into a dirt track, then climbs to the ridge where you can ride cross-country to the Gran Piedra, the highest mountain in the area.

The next day we opt for the paved route to Gran Piedra. We ride along the quiet country club road, my butt sore from all the cycling (Mel's is "fine," she says). We pass the palm-lined club that is now a protocol house that members of the military can use for visiting foreign guests, then turn onto Calle Siboney. I grind up the long Sevilla hill, past monuments to the revolutionaries killed in the attack on the Moncada barracks. Melissa and Reg wait at the top, then we fly down the other side to Granjita Siboney.

The dirt track to Gran Piedra, which we drive the next day, climbs a grueling 1,214 metres in 14 kilometres. To the left and right, perfect mountain-biking tracks wind past coffee plantations and abandoned gold mines. The pine-scented air is a refreshing change from the steaming city. Three-quarters of all of Cuba's trees are found here, and 222 varieties of ground plants. Leo, whose teased platinum blonde hair and Lycra-clad body belie her upbringing on a farm, collects medicinal herbs along the way. Climbing another 70 metres on foot to the top of Gran Piedra, we look out over the hazel-coloured hills to the blue mountains of Jamaica beyond.

Reg leads us to the *autopista* and up a six-kilometre hill to the sugar cane–growing area of El Cristo. He and Melissa wait for me under the "Defendemos Nuestras Conquistas" (Defend

Our Conquests) sign exhorting Cubans to defend what they've achieved: literacy, health care for all. On the descent, I pass two Cuban men on one-speeds. "Change bikes?" one asks, peddling beside me on his Flying Pigeon. I shake my head. "Is that girl married?" asks the other of my sister, who has just passed him. He is her age, late thirties, handsome.

"No," I say, "she isn't."

"*Ella esta muy fuerte.*"

"Yes," I say. "She is. Very strong."

Postscript:

When she tells me she's leaving Jerko, I'm ecstatic.

"Our trip gave me the courage to go," she says. "Men liked me. They were nice to me."

That was all it took—an island living in the past, warm-hearted, flirtatious men, and a week of doing something she is very good at—to free her. Worth being left behind. Worth every minute.

DOS CAMINOS

I HAVE A FILE on the Cuban boy Elián Gonzalez. Articles, interviews, photographs about the trip he and his mother took in 1999 with ten other people on a small raft. How a storm hit, and all died except Elián and two others. Elián was found floating in the Florida Straits. Age five. Two days alone. His mother left Cuba with the boy, without telling his father, her ex-husband Juan Miguel.

In the American newspaper, he walks to school with his great-uncle Lazaro, his small hand swallowed by the big one. In another, a black dog pulls him toward the camera. Elián's hand, the one that is unleashed, is open, his eyes watchful.

In the Cuban newspaper *Granma*, Elián and his father clap at the antics of a clown in an old photo. Fidel, in army fatigues, addresses Elián's classmates; an old woman brandishes a placard: *Queremos a Elián en Cuba*. We want Elián in Cuba.

As I turn the pages of my file, I think of Pedro. I met him in Santa Cruz, Bolivia, an agricultural city in the eastern jungle, where I'd gone to visit my friend Richard. Richard and Pedro are Cuban. Both teach at Bolivian universities. Both left a country where a university professor earns twenty dollars a month, where unless you have access to tourist dollars or overseas remittances, it is difficult to support a family. To survive on what the ration card provides: bread, sugar, eggs, coffee, *chícharos* (beans) from Canada.

Pedro was born in Dos Caminos (Two Roads), a small city in eastern Cuba. A town I'd cycled through several months earlier. He was a *brigadista*, a teacher in the great Cuban literacy campaign of 1961, the *Campaña Nacional de Alfabetización*. Over a hundred thousand student volunteers were dispatched to the countryside to teach *campesinos* to read and write. Pedro taught in the Sierra Maestra, the birthplace of the revolution. He also cut sugar cane alongside Che Guevara, built schools and hospitals, spoke fluent Russian. He was, he said, "a revolution man." Guevara's New Man.

Richard and Pedro had different teaching schedules so when one was in class the other would escort me around this green and steamy city. We visited churches and the few museums Santa Cruz had to offer, but mostly we ate at restaurants. One evening, we went with a group of Cuban professors to a café called Dumbos where we ordered Cuban sandwiches, huge crusty rolls stuffed with pork, ham, beef, and chicken. "Ha ha," the Cubans joked, "these Bolivians obviously don't know that in Cuba, we only eat meat twice a year."

My friends bantered about the laziness of their wealthy students, the variety of things you could buy in Bolivia. "It is one big market," they proclaimed. They also spoke longingly of the ballet and concerts, the seafront boulevard of Havana called the Malecón; shared news from the latest *Granma* newspaper, gossiped about the minister removed from office; talked of the televisions and clothes they would send back home.

I was never allowed to pay for these meals. At the Brazilian buffets, Pedro would urge me to fill my plate, two, three times. At the *parrilladas* or barbeque restaurants, Richard ordered platter after platter of grilled meat, urged me to forgo the vegetables, "*come la carne.*" Eat the meat.

One day Pedro and I went shopping for a present for Richard's birthday. We sauntered down one of the main shopping streets lined with stalls selling fruit, vegetables, clothes, dishes, auto parts, jewellery. He told me Richard wanted a good watch; the ones he bought from street hawkers stopped working after a few days. We examined Casios, Timexes. "Which is a good brand?" Pedro asked of the dizzying array. "Which one is best?" We settled on a slim, silver Casio with a blue face. The clerk told us a price and Pedro nodded. "Too much," I said, suggesting half. I smiled at Pedro, thinking his PhD in Marxist economics wasn't much help outside Cuba as he hadn't learned yet to barter.

After shopping, we stopped at one of the ubiquitous Bolivian *pollo a la brasa* restaurants. Over drumsticks and beer, Pedro told me about his life in Havana. Before the Soviets pulled out in 1990, ending their subsidies of the Cuban economy, Pedro was a senior professor. He had a house, two cars, annual vacation paid for by the state. "My wife and I would go to Guanabo beach east of Havana. Walk on the beautiful white sands, eat fish in an open-air restaurant, dance at a—how do you call it?—*cabaña*, at night under stars. My wife is a beautiful dancer."

Then Fidel announced the special period. There was no gas, he was given a Chinese Forever bicycle and told to ride the thirty-five kilometres to work. If he didn't like it, he could take a *camello*, the large, crowded buses pulled by transport trucks. "And then the government gave the beaches to the tourists, and now only the *jineteras*, the Cuban girls with their foreign men, can afford to stay at resorts there."

His wife got sick. There are good doctors in Cuba, Pedro told me, but no medicine because of the U.S. embargo. He wrote to distant relatives in Spain and the United States, asking for medicine. Finally, he was forced to take a job in Bolivia, where he must give 75 percent of his wages to the Cuban government but earns enough money to buy the medication his wife needs.

His eyes look beyond the fluorescent lights and honking cars in the street, back to the days he and his wife danced salsa, walked the Malecón. The same seawall I had cycled months earlier, waves crashing over it, drenching me. At night, the lights of the hotels would wink then vanish as my taxi flew into the tunnel beneath the Almendares River, emerging to the crumbing yellow mansions and gardens of Miramar. I imagine Pedro and his wife dangling their legs over the stone seawall, looking across the bay to the Morro Castle guarding the entrance to the harbour, to the fortress, La Cabaña, where Che and Fidel plotted the country's future.

A few months ago in Calgary, I went with Mercedes, Richard's sister, and her husband to see *The Buena Vista Social Club*. They whispered, "There's the Malecón, El Capitolio, the Plaza of the Revolution," grew excited when they saw the famous Coppelia ice cream shop. Outside the theatre, their ten-year-old son, who has lived half his life in Canada, asked, "Why were there so many people in the street in the movie? What were they staring at?"

The future, Arielito, I wanted to say, Carnegie Hall and the Statue of Liberty and everything you could possibly want in the stores. Or the past—where the electricity is not just for tourist hotels, where you could listen to the records of Benny Moré and Arsenio Rodríguez, roast a pig in your backyard and hold a party for all your neighbours, drink rum and dance all night. But I know I was just a romanticizing tourist in Cuba, not subject to the everyday sweat of trying to make a living, find food, soap, medicine.

In the *pollo a la brasa*, which I discovered means rotisserie chicken, I watched Pedro, the revolutionary man, reminisce, tears in his eyes, looking at the bones of his chicken. Stuck in this country of markets and meat, so far from home.

Later, he walked me to the bus station, steering me past street children selling bread, pan dulce, sweet bread. I wanted to go to La Higuera, the place where Che Guevara, having tried to export the revolution to Bolivia, was captured by the army and shot by a Bolivian soldier on the dirt floor of the local schoolhouse. Shot, then taken to the hospital at Vallegrande, where his hands were cut off and he lay, surrounded by Bolivian and American soldiers and reporters, handless, eyes rolled heavenward. I wanted to go to La Higuera or Vallegrande but it was too hard, three bus changes. Besides, I was told at the bus station, there is nothing there. Just bad roads and poor people.

Months earlier, cycling down the wide boulevard of Dos Caminos, Pedro's hometown, I'd seen a billboard of Che's words: "*No hay tareas difíciles si no hay hombres incapaces.*" There are no difficult works if men are not incapacitated. And in nearby San Luis: "My Cuban heart has faith in victory."

At home, I pour over the newspapers, looking for news of Elián. United States Attorney General Janet Reno has ordered his return to Cuba. He is taken by force from his relative's home in Miami. In a picture from Cuba, he and his father smile, his father's arm draped protectively around his neck. In another, crowds in the Plaza of the Revolution wave placards: "Elián, my friend, we are with you." Though Mercedes says a joke circulating in Cuba is "Elián, my friend, take me with you."

I think of Mercedes and Richard's mother, Caridad, whom I visited in Havana. A pile of rice in front of her on the kitchen table, Caridad carefully picking out small black stones. The meals she made for me: soup with *chícharos*; flan with her precious ration-card eggs, fruit salad. Nights when there weren't black- or brown-outs, she and I watched the Colombian soap opera *Coffee with the Aroma of a Woman*, or the trial of the Salvadoran man accused of planting bombs in tourist hotels, one of which killed a *turista*. Hired, according the newsman, by Cuban-Americans, to destroy the revolution.

There were two roads Elián's life could take. One in the United States, where he could eat meat, he could eat cake, go to Disneyland, play Nintendo. And the one in Cuba, in Cárdenas with his father and grandparents, where he will have a free education, access to doctors though maybe not medicine, will be taught to study, do volunteer work, run through the streets with a torch on José Martí day, ride a Forever bicycle past signs exhorting him to work hard like Che. He will memorize the details of all the revolutionary battles, learn to dance salsa. He will eat *chícharos* from Canada with his father. Swim with his grandmothers.

On one website, I find a close-up of Elián in a crisp white shirt. At the edge of the picture, the arm and gold watch of his Great-uncle Lazaro are visible.

Richard's American watch hasn't stopped. It is ticking down the time to when he and Pedro can return home, to their families, to their beloved country. While little Elián's eyes stare straight ahead, into the unknowable.

Postscript:
Elián Gonzalez and Fidel Castro became lifelong friends after the boy returned to Cuba. Elián joined the Young Communist League at age fourteen and trained as an industrial engineer. He was elected a member of Cuba's National Assembly in 2023.

A TALE OF TWO TENTS

> *"WARNING: Women tourists should not in any circumstances take tours on their own or in pairs with independent guides but should stick to larger group tours run by reputable agencies."*
>
> —"Bolivian Jungle Tours," www.lonelyplanet.com

WE DRIFT TOWARD the camp spot just as dusk is settling on the brown Ibare River. Fish splash the still water. Papacho noses the boat into the bank then jumps out to haul it in. I scan for the crocodiles I've seen all afternoon slipping down the mud and into the water. Papacho motions me out and we hike to a clearing on the edge of the jungle where we will spend the night.

It's dark when Papacho begins setting up a tiny pup tent. Where is mine? I ask, having insisted on two tents when I hired him in the jungle town of Trinidad in eastern Bolivia to take me up this tributary of the Mamoré River. One tent is better, he says. One tent is not better, I say. You will be frightened, he says. I will not be frightened, I say. There are caiman, jaguar, bear, he says. My country is full of bears, I say. We haven't passed a single boat all day. We are miles from anywhere.

I know nothing about this man except that his sister runs the hostel where I stayed. That exactly one waiter and one travel agent said he was a good guide.

I wandered the dusty streets of Trinidad looking for other backpackers who might want to ply a river. For days, I sat in the ice cream parlour at the edge of the plaza, watching cars and motorcycles roar by and listening to sound systems trying to out-"La Vida Loca" each other. Listening to church bells which rang for ten minutes, took a break for five, and resumed on the quarter hour, I searched for tourists among tidy families who strolled the plaza, knots of teenagers at the *heladería*, but found no one.

Well, there was one other woman. A Frenchwoman I'd see striding around town or out to the Laguna Suárez in a pair of long hiking shorts, button-down shirt, wool knee socks, and safari hat. She was heading to Guayaramerín but told me she'd met a New Zealand couple who wanted to do a river trip. They, however, eluded me.

I debated with myself: You've come all this way to go on the river, just hire him; it's stupid to go on your own. Papacho seems like a nice guy; what about the German girl who was attacked by her guide in Rurrenabaque? He doesn't speak English; a great opportunity to practise your Spanish. You've been travelling for six months and nothing bad has happened to you; what about the bus hijacking in Mexico? That was years ago and it was because you took a night bus. Shut up, I told the voices, and over yet another dish of chocolate ice cream, I wrote down the pros and cons. The pros won. So I hired Papacho to take me down the river.

The first day of our trip came. As did Papacho, two hours late, on a borrowed motorcycle with no gear. *Desafortunadamente* his friend had borrowed the motor from his boat to go fishing. He would take me to the town of Loreto to see the old Jesuit mission instead, and we would be on the river early the next day. We bumped down dusty roads, stopping to look at jabiru storks, egrets, and heron on the pampas. An anteater ran across our path, forcing Papacho to slam on the brakes and me to crash into his back.

Maybe it was me holding on to his waist tightly as other motorcycles and trucks roared by pelting us with stones and dust that gave him the one-tent idea. Or maybe it was because I bought him a beer in Loreto while we ate *gallina picante*, hen with hot sauce, as their sisters pecked the scrubby yard. Or maybe it was just because I was a *gringa* alone.

The next day, motor restored, we set off. Just me, Papacho, and Gabriel García Márquez—in the form of a tattered copy of *One Hundred Years of Solitude*, the story of seven generations of the Buendía family in the remote town of Macondo and one hundred years of Colombian history. I swung in the hammock Papacho had rigged for me, alternately watching the river and reading, smugly thinking it fitting that I was reading a book set in a remote jungle town while travelling through remote jungle. Would we, like José Arcadio Buendía, discover a Spanish galleon rooted in stone, a lushness of flowers and trees growing inside it? José Arcadio thought he had found a town surrounded by water on all sides. I was surrounded by water on all sides. Every so often Papacho called *Mira* and I'd look up to see the roseate fin of a *bufeo,* a pink dolphin, disappearing into brown, or a stork, its long legs hanging brokenly, cutting across the sky over the river.

We stopped for a midday lunch of piranha and hiked to a lagoon. The air was close. Papacho cut through the undergrowth with his machete until we got to the edge of the lagoon. "If a caiman attacks you," he said, "dive underneath it." Absolutely.

We stopped for an afternoon swim. "*Hay cocodrilos aqui?*" I asked. "No," Papacho said, adding that they only attack people when they're very hungry. I noticed he was in and out of the tea-coloured water in record time. I followed suit, retreating to my hammock where Colonel Aureliano had decided to retreat from the world to become an alchemist, to fashion tiny fish out of gold.

Maybe the tent problem was just miscommunication. Papacho didn't speak English. I found his Spanish hard to understand and perhaps he found mine the same. Maybe I wasn't using the right words. The word for tent, *tienda,* also means store. The other word for tent, *carpa,* also means carp. I'd asked, "Hay dos tiendas? Hay dos carpas?" Are there two tents? Are there two stores? Are there two fish? Or perhaps I'd said, "Muy necesito mi propia carpa," I really need my own carp. He'd answered, *Si, claro,* meaning, perhaps, that he'd bring his fishing rod, he'd catch me one.

Or perhaps he had expectations. Did the gringas he brought down this river come to his *tienda* in the middle of the night, like the women who'd silently slip into the tent of the war hero Colonel Aureliano to partake of his genetic bounty?

Papacho disappeared over the bank. Huddling in the dark and slapping at mosquitoes, the voices in my head resumed: You can sleep in the boat; so can the crocodiles. You can take the boat; good luck starting the motor, it takes Papacho ten minutes. He's been nice so far; you don't even know him.

I shiver in the dark, slap mosquitoes, put on a sweater. What the heck is Papacho doing down there? Just as I decide I'll sleep in the boat, crocodiles or no crocodiles, he appears with a flashlight and a rolled-up tarp. You sure you want your own tent? he asks. "*Absoluto*," I say. I think I'm saying absolutely but I could also be saying pure alcohol. He smiles as if to say *You can't blame a guy for trying*, unrolls the tarp, and pulls out a second tent. As we shake it out, my shoulders and stomach muscles unclench. Just as they did when the hijackers finished robbing us and left us lying on the cold ground in the middle of a Mexican field. As the stomachs of the women of Macondo did when their husbands returned from the wars.

Outside this ring of light, a dolphin jumps, crocodiles slide in and out of the water below. Something snorts. A bear? A caiman? The patron saint of careless *gringas*? Papacho himself, perhaps?

ESPÍRITU SANTO

THE WIND HOWLED across the Sea of Cortez, brewing waves and hurling them against my kayak. Four others bobbed ahead of me like beads on a broken necklace. I hauled on my paddle, pulled the water. Should be pushing. Save my back. The jagged coast of Isla Partida, our destination, was as far away as ever. Whitecaps washed over the side. I rode a trough, emerged sideways. Waves slapped my boat, threatened to tip. Paddling madly, I straightened out.

The wet exit—how did Francisco, our guide, say it went? Release the spray skirt. Slide out. Hang onto the kayak. Blow your whistle.

Salt water broke over my bow, drenching my arms and spray skirt. I sat in a pool of cold water, my mouth dry, but I didn't dare stop paddling to drink. It was all I could do to stay upright. Somewhere behind me was Francisco. The rest of our group were ahead. Normally Mel would be way out in front, but out of respect for Francisco's request that we all stay together, she was holding back her inner Amazon.

A sudden blast of wind pushed at my boat, rolling it to one side. I shifted my weight, overcorrected, and almost dumped. Even though I wasn't a beginner, I didn't feel at all prepared for the rigours of this crossing. Was I getting too old for this type of adventure?

Two days before, Mel and I arrived in La Paz, the capital of Baja California Sur, the long, peninsular Mexican state that dangles into the Pacific like a continental afterthought. La Paz lies near the Baja's southeast tip, across the Gulf of California from mainland Mexico. It sits on the edge of a bay guarded by Espíritu Santo (Holy Spirit) Island. We're here to embark on a seven-day circumnavigation of the island, through waters known more poetically as the Sea of Cortez. These waters were made famous by John Steinbeck in his book *The Log from the Sea of Cortez.* Espíritu Santo is volcanic and comprises both the main island and smaller Isla Partida, which is connected to it by a narrow isthmus, collectively thirty-two kilometres from north to south and ten kilometres across at its widest. It contains the most intact ecosystem in the region, including many endemic plant species and a black-tailed jackrabbit found nowhere else.

Bought by an ecological consortium and transferred to the Mexican government, it is part of a Mexican flora and fauna protection area and has been designated a UNESCO biosphere reserve.

For a day, Mel and I explored La Paz, walking along the Malecón, a wide, tiled path that stretches for miles along the Bahía de la Paz where the local paceños, as the residents of La Paz are called, gather to watch the sunset, play soccer or volleyball on the beach, jog or walk in large family groups. That day most were swathed in track suits, toques, and scarves against the wind that blew in with the twenty-degree cold front, the *frente frio*. In the evening, we sat in the dark, deserted bar of our hotel, peering at a picture book of the Baja while we waited for our guide from Baja Outdoor Adventures to arrive and prep us for our trip. Francisco arrived precisely on time, a tanned, muscled forty-one-year-old with closely cropped hair and narrow brown eyes bracketed by crow's feet.

"Tomorrow I will pick up the rest of our group in the van, then we will cross from La Paz to Coralito Bay on Espíritu Santo Island in the skiff. The crossing will be about forty-five minutes. The kayaks will be there waiting for us. We will paddle north, up the west coast of the island, cross to Isla Partida, then come back and paddle down the east coast of Espíritu Santo, moving to a new camp spot each night."

"It seems very windy," I said. "Will that affect our trip?"

Francisco smiled. "Not if we leave early."

I remembered the crossing Mel and I had made thirteen years before in 1997, to Isla Coronado, further north in this same sea. We were in a double kayak, and I had to steer because my tall, athletic sister's legs were too long for the rudder. The wind was fierce, pushing our boat around, capping the waves. If we didn't make a landing on the island, we'd be pushed out to sea, no other islands to head for, no protection.

"Paddle," I'd yelled at my sister, above the wind's roar.

"You paddle!" she screamed back.

"I'm trying to steer us. Keep us from tipping. Shit!" I said as a wave drenched me. "Go, damn it."

"I'm paddling as hard as I can."

"You're not!"

"Shut up!"

"You shut up." And then, I don't know why I did it, the adrenalin, the fear, hunger, the distant and seemingly unreachable island, I hit my sister over the head with my paddle. Lightly, I've always said in my defence, to urge her to greater feats of strength. I won't repeat what we screamed at each other. When we finally made the landing, our *compañeros* rushed out to pull us to shore.

My sister has never forgotten this incident. She reminds me of it regularly. It's just a matter of time before Francisco hears about it.

Francisco's dream, he said, was to "get lost" somewhere in Central Asia. He'd left a life as a lawyer in Chile to travel and work as a guide. He'd hiked the Pacific Crest Trail from Mexico to Canada, led kayak trips in Greenland and Patagonia, and canoed remote lakes in Northern Ontario. Over the course of the evening, he told us about his travels, about a Québécois ex-girlfriend and an American ex-girlfriend; I suspected he had a girlfriend, or ex-girlfriend, in every port, that he would no doubt have one in the outer reaches of Inner Mongolia or the inner reaches of Outer Mongolia or wherever it was that he was lost. I could understand how a woman might succumb to his charms.

Chileans, Francisco told us that first night in the hotel bar, have the same relationship to time that the Brits have to drink. They respect it. Sure enough, the following morning, he arrived promptly on time and introduced Mel and me to the people who would be our companions for the next seven days: Alvaro, our cook, a smiling, rotund paceño; Mario, our boat driver, tanned, fit, and solicitous; Jack and his wife, Elaine, a former journalist from New York City now working for the town of Crested Butte, Colorado, where they spend their winters skiing. Jack was a laid-back, ponytailed former Californian, a commercial fisherman in summer. He went to Berkeley, served in the navy in Vietnam. ("Didn't see the bad stuff," he said, "otherwise I'd be a different person today.")

They moved to Alaska in the sixties, built themselves what Eileen lovingly referred to as the "shackteau," and lived on the land. The other couple who was to be with us for the first four days, Sue and Roy, were from Penticton, British Columbia. A former ski-tour leader, she was chatty, already sorting out where we were from, who was married, who had children, what we did. Roy was quiet, though later he told us that he'd recently sold his construction company for a tidy sum and had taken early retirement.

The first day, after a wild and bumpy skiff crossing from La Paz, we landed at Coralito Bay in the middle of the west side of the island, launched the kayaks, and paddled north toward Candelero Bay. I was worried about my ability to kayak all day. I'd kayaked occasionally on day trips with Mel, on the West Coast and on the Baja trip thirteen years ago, but I was unsure about my ability to keep up with the more experienced in the group—anxious about how my body, my neck and shoulders, those tension-holding, migraine-triggerers, would do. Indeed, after only an hour of pulling the paddle, my forearms and shoulders were aching.

"My arms are killing me," I told Francisco as he paddled up beside me. "What am I doing wrong?"

"Loosen that grip on the paddle. Hold it lightly, like this." He twirled his through his fingers. "Now push it forward rather than pulling." I watched his back move back and forth. "Find and use your abs for strength."

"I don't believe I have abs."

"I'm sure you do."

"Perhaps I've just misplaced them then."

Once I got the rhythm and resigned myself to being near the back of the group, I found the paddling didn't require much thinking at all. I could stare up at the tall poles of cordon cacti and blood-orange volcanic cliffs of the barren island rising straight as fortress walls from the ocean. I watched blue herons perched still as museum guards on the edge of small rocks, a foot drawn into their bodies. Frigate birds with their red chin pouches, cormorants and black vultures wheeled around the wide sky. A school of flying fish. Jumping dolphins. In the distance, a breaching whale.

On Isla Partida, we set up our tents on the yellow sand beach at Ensenada Grande, away from "Paco," our chemical toilet, whose hidden location was signalled by a blue dry bag. Mario and Francisco had set up a large tarp, and under it, white plastic stubby-legged chairs and a large ice-filled cooler with drinks. Nearby, Alvaro presided over his cooking area: two wooden tables, a large Coleman stove, containers of food hauled from the skiff.

The next morning, Francisco led us on a hike up a dusty trail, past skinny, multi-armed pitahaya cacti and flat, paddle-shaped prickly pear cacti to an old well. It was built during the Second World War to provide water for Mexican soldiers stationed there to protect the peninsula against Japanese invasion. The Mexican government had refused an American offer of troops ("They remembered the Alamo," said Francisco). He told us about the nomadic, native Pericú, descended, some say, from Polynesians who fished on the island. They had gone now, leaving only their pictographs.

One of which we saw on another day. We landed on a narrow beach where local spear fishermen—modern-day nomads—dozed in the sun, and we climbed craggy, rust-coloured boulders to a box canyon. Francisco told us to look up, and we all scanned the rock for the ancient tortoise he had seen there before. Francisco found it and we clustered around, staring. It was high up, just where a hand could reach: a simple, recognizable ochre print.

I AM FASCINATED BY nomads. Bruce Chatwin walking the songlines with Aboriginal people in Australia; Robyn Davidson travelling with the Rabari shepherds in Gujarat, India; Alexandra David-Néel disguising herself as a pilgrim and stealing into a Tibet closed to the outside world. I'm drawn to the idea of going where other travellers haven't, the idea of getting lost, though I've travelled enough to know the "gringo trail" is very wide, that we are everywhere. Francisco wanted to blend in with the natives in Mongolia, and with his tanned skin, his self-proclaimed "Chinese eyes," maybe he did. There's no blending for me. Blue eyes, fair skin, peeling, sunburned nose, glasses.

In Cuba, when I took a *botero* (the local peso taxi) I was told to hide when we passed a policeman, so clearly was I not a Cubana. On a bus in Bolivia, the other passengers huddled around me so that the police officer we passed wouldn't notice a white face and stop the bus to demand my passport, slowing its already glacial progress. In Istanbul, the carpet sellers called out, "Hello, Canadian lady" when I passed. They recognized the MEC label, I later learned.

But now, in my late forties, perhaps the time for such great adventures has passed. Though Alexandra David-Néel was my age when she first walked into Tibet. Dervla Murphy, the Irish travel writer in her seventies, is still roaming the lonelier reaches of our planet. And my octogenarian parents are still willing to endure bone-jarring bus rides to hike through the midday heat to remote Turkish archeological sites or to visit a Huichol village in the Sierra Madres in Mexico. Just as they endured a carful of squabbling children, driving the back roads in the Kootenays, looking for ghost towns, searching for pictographs to show us.

MEL AND I WERE getting along perfectly on this trip. I hadn't yet hit her with my paddle; she wasn't nagging me to keep up with her; our different wake-up times (hers five, mine seven or later) weren't an issue because breakfast was early; and we couldn't argue about who was on whose side because we each had our own tent. She could be snoring away by nine p.m. and I could read late into the night. I'd wondered how we would do in such close quarters for a week. She needed to be on the move; I had to have time to read, write, observe. Even so, she was more relaxed, while I was energized by this desert landscape, which we agreed reminded us of our hometown, Kamloops.

As kids we'd hike the cactus-covered hills behind our house, armed with sandwiches, a thermos of water, and instructions to look after our two little sisters and be home for dinner. We'd arrive back at six, hot, filthy, and exhausted, our heads filled with what we had seen: a field of mariposa lilies, a storm of tumbleweed, an arrowhead, burrs and cacti thorns sticking to our socks.

As teenagers we fought. Physically, scratching and hitting each other. With words. I don't even remember what we fought about, but when our parents were out, we screamed at each other, hit, kicked, so violently that once our little sisters ran to the neighbours for help. She was shy, brainy, gangly. She was two years younger and six inches taller than me. We competed in everything: grades, tennis. I beat her at tennis. She beat me at school.

On Espíritu Santo, Mel and I woke up covered in sandfly and chigger bites, happy and ready for Alvaro's huevos rancheros and cinnamon-flavoured coffee. We rose to sunrises the colour of tangerines, the inner petal of a wild rose. To beaches deserted except for our lonely tents. In a place that was, as Jack called it, "a little piece of paradise."

In the afternoons, Francisco would move between Mario and Alvaro, who sat at the card table listening to norteño music on Alvaro's little radio, and the paying customers. He joked and sang with the Mexicans then returned to sit with us, gearing the conversation to our areas of interest, providing information about the history and geography of the desert landscape of the Baja when he saw we were intrigued.

Archeologists, he said, have found evidence in caves on Espíritu Santo of inhabitants living here thirty to forty thousand years ago. Ancestors of the Pericú may have migrated here across the Pacific and not across the Bering Strait from Siberia as previously thought. The conquistador Hernán Cortés encountered Pericú on an expedition to the Baja in the 1530s. Two centuries later, the Jesuits established missions in the southern cape area, including at La Paz. In 1734, the seagoing Pericú revolted, killing two missionaries, after a Jesuit padre passed an injunction against polygamy.

After four days of kayaking, Sue and Roy left us for a spa at La Paz, and we were joined by Sharon from Los Angeles, fresh from finishing a PhD in education. We had late afternoon discussions about the state of the world, the horrors of Bush II, the benefits of "socialized medicine." We told her about the day we went swimming with the sea lions at Los Islotes, the sleek brown bodies of the young males diving off the rocks and gliding soundlessly alongside us. Startling, dangerous perhaps, but beautiful.

Alvaro was steaming tamales. We smelled the warm corn dough as we settled into our legless plastic chairs after a day of paddling, to read or write in our diaries. Jack and I were reading the same book: *The Glass Castle*, a memoir by Jeannette Wells, who grew up in poverty with artistic, eccentric parents who were utterly inept at providing for the material needs of their children but instilled in them a love of learning, thinking, dreaming. She wrote of their nomadic life, traipsing from place to place—the California desert, Phoenix, West Virginia—leaving each one when the debts piled up, or her father went on a bender and lost his job.

She loved the desert the most.

I've been lost, I tell our group. In the Bolivian Yungas, the donkey-driver/guide and the young Israeli ex-army guys I was trekking with left me in the dust (well, scree). I went down the wrong valley and had to cross a steep ridge to the next, stumbled down rock in the falling dusk, cursing like a soldier myself and stumbling into camp in the dark. My companions were high on adrenaline and the beauty of the mountain lake we'd trekked to, oblivious to my anger.

I've been stranded. In 1989, my sister Jocelyn and I were travelling from Srinagar to Leh, India, in a bus that was grounded by a freak snowstorm in the Shia Muslim village of Kargil. The village had little food, and was the site of border skirmishes with Pakistan. We spent days in bed in our unheated hotel room, reading Lama Anagarika Govinda's

The Way of the White Clouds, Alexandra David-Néel's *My Journey to Lhasa*, and Heinrich Harrer's *Seven Years in Tibet* aloud to each other, portioning out the books like the bits of Amul processed cheese and the few dry biscuits we had for nourishment. After a week, a bus made it through from Srinagar to pick up stranded passengers. We didn't want to go back to Srinagar. So, with an Austrian mountain climber who was travelling to Leh to scatter his climbing partner's ashes, my sister and I hired a taxi. A taxi that we had to push through ice and water, around rocks and power lines bent to the ground by snow to get to Leh.

In 1924, Alexandra David-Néel disguised herself as a beggarwoman to sneak into that mystical, isolated mountain country. Ladakh was teeming with military bases, with soldiers guarding the border with China, and we weren't that adventurous or that brave.

In his seven years as a kayak guide in the Baja, Francisco has only seen ten days of rain. Eleven, including this, our second-last day. He'd left his rain gear hanging in his closet at home. As had I.

Ocean and sky blended together, a lavender-grey, the rain ebbing and flowing from a steady downpour to a gentle spit. We paddled through an old pearling area, Bahía San Gabriel, near the south end of western Espíritu Santo. I read that the Pericú dived for these pearls. Many died in combat and others died from Old World diseases such as smallpox, syphilis, and measles. By 1768, when the Spanish crown expelled the Jesuits from the Baja, the Pericú were mostly extinct.

In the sixteenth century, pearl fishermen from mainland Mexico worked the rich beds here. The pearl beds of Espíritu Santo were some of the richest in the Gulf, and poor fishermen armed with spears dove, hoping to find, as Steinbeck described it in his novella *The Pearl*, the "pearl of the world." By the 1940s, when Steinbeck and Ricketts made their marine collecting trip in the Sea of Cortez, pearling had all but died out, a victim of overdiving and diseased oysters.

In a light rain, we glided silently past mangroves dotted with black frigate birds, their scarlet pouches furled, then we continued farther along the narrow bay into a red mangrove area. We guided our kayaks down narrow passages between the overhanging bushes, the sides bumping against the myriad of reddy-brown roots. I remembered canoeing in the Everglades of Florida with Mel and my then-boyfriend Lindsay. I was in front, Mel in the middle, and Lins at the back. Lins didn't know how to steer the canoe properly and we kept bumping into the sides of the narrow channel we were paddling. We passed alligators sunning themselves on the banks, heard their plop into the water, saw their snouts as they swam across.

"Gators up ahead, go left, LEFT," I ordered.

"I'm trying."

"Okay, pull along the bank there, I'll steer."

I'm not sure what made me think I could do any better than he was doing except I was twenty-two and thought I could do anything. I'm not sure what made me hit my sister over the head with a paddle fourteen years later except I was thirty-six and was beginning to realize I couldn't.

Later that day, we pulled into our new camp at Playa Dispensa, shivered out of our wet clothes and into dry, warm ones. We sat in our dwarf chairs under the tarp and drank Mayan sacrifices (milk, tequila, and coffee liqueur). I perused the "library," which was housed in a large orange waterproof box, chose a book on Mexican proverbs, and started reading.

Mel asked me to read with my lips closed. I hit her (playfully, and with fist not paddle). Funny girl!

"*Qué bonito es ver llover y no mojarse.*" How beautiful to watch the rain and not get wet, I thought.

Jack came back from a walk to Paco. Behind the beach, he told us, there was a site out of Hitchcock's *The Birds*. Mel and I went to look. Thousands of zopilotes—buzzards—were perched on the tops of giant cordon cacti, wings fanned to each side, drying in the orange dusk. We stood there entranced. The sight was eerie, ethereal, strangely beautiful.

On our last day, the desert bloomed. Overnight, little shrubs had sprouted leaves and tiny red blossoms on their tips. The pitahaya, the cholla, the prickly pear, tall century plants were green. Cacti sprouted small white flowers. The desert, Francisco told us, would be at its best next week. But this was our last day. Mud squelched under our shoes, threatening to pull them off as we walked toward the hill separating two beaches, Playa la Bonanza on the east side of southern Espíritu Santo and Bahía San Gabriel on the west side. We climbed *las faldas* (how much more poetic is the Spanish "skirts" than the English "sides") to the top. We gazed at San Gabriel Bay where we would be picked up by the skiff that afternoon to head back to Bonanza Beach.

At San Gabriel, we swam and ate lunch. We packed the skiff. Manuel arrived with the big boat to take us back to La Paz on the mainland. We ate the ice cream that Manuel had brought from town. There was nothing left to do, but no one wanted to leave. We went for a final swim, took a last walk on the beach, made one final trip to Paco. It was way past Chilean and Canadian and American and Mexican leaving time. Still we stayed.

Francisco told us that when he left his job as a lawyer in Chile, his family and friends didn't understand. They still don't, he said.

A friend once said to me: "I never could figure out why you were always going off to places where you didn't speak the language or know anyone. But I figured it out. You like to be on the outside looking in. You like to be alone."

When Mel and I first kayaked in the Baja, one of the guides seemed more interested in perfecting his own kayaking skills than assisting us, and one of the women kayakers retreated to her tent the minute we hit the beach and didn't talk to anyone. We had our fight. I fell in love with the Baja's desert landscape, the barren red volcanic cliffs, the canyons, the cacti, the silence. I made a vow to return.

On that trip, I read Graham Mackintosh's *Into a Desert Place*, a 1988 account of walking three thousand miles around the Baja, by himself for much of the time then with a burro named Bonnie. He was young, and had rarely ventured from his small, English working-class town before the trip. He wrote: "I thought back to the first mile I walked from San Felipe, and how alone and frightened I felt in the face of a burning vastness that seemed to be mocking each pathetic little step along the sand. I had carried on because I felt that I was answering the call of something much bigger than my fears. And here I was. In an hour or two the end would be in sight. Then I would have the rest of my life to try to figure out what it was all about."

Back in La Paz, we dispersed, Sharon to her hotel on the Malecón, and Jack, Eileen, Mel, and me to our hotel, El Angel Azul, to wash the sea from our clothes. Later, we tripped on our sea legs down the dark, crumbling streets to meet the others for dinner. Francisco entertained us with a story about a trip on the French River in Ontario.

"There were two couples and a girl who was supposed to be experienced but she couldn't paddle. She kept going in circles."

"What did you do?" we asked.

"I had to tow her."

"For how long?"

"The whole trip. The other couples kept telling her she was getting better, but she wasn't. I had no choice."

We laughed, thinking at least we knew how to paddle, didn't have to be towed. Graham, in his walk around the Baja, depended on the kindness of strangers, fishermen who shared their catches with him when he was out of food, tourists who gave him clothes and food and beer and water. I didn't have to be towed, but people helped me, too, on my travels: the Argentinian farmer who chased down a boy who stole my backpack, the tailors in Srinagar who fed Jocelyn and me and invited us to their family home. No one travels alone. No one journeys without help. Alexandra David-Néel had a rich husband to finance her travels. I had money. On this trip, I had a shy but strong sister.

Mel and I gave Francisco our addresses, invited him to stay if he was ever out our way. I'd teach him to ski, take him to the Rockies' best cross-country ski trails; Mel would take him cycling to the hidden treasures of Vancouver Island, in return for the little piece of paradise he'd shown us. Then we said our goodbyes, and everyone was gone.

The next day, Mel and I got on a bus to Todos Santos. We trolled the dusty streets, past groups of package tourists up from Cabo San Lucas for the day. Past art galleries and souvenir shops, the church, the *zocalo* (central plaza). The town was full of roaring pickups but there was not a taxi or a room under two hundred dollars a night to be found.

We finally secured a room, Mel and I, on the top floor of a quiet surfer hotel outside of town, where we sat on the balcony in loving silence, watching the sun disappear behind the trees, and in the red spread of dusk, birds coming to rest on the treetops. Listening to the distant sea.

AUTISTIC IN CEBU

KIDS IN GREEN UNIFORMS are lined up, three abreast, in the open cement courtyard of the school. The sound system has been set up beside the guard's desk. Someone pushes the play button and Karen Carpenter's "Top of the World" blasts from the speakers. Teacher Aubrey begins the morning exercises. She can't resist adding a little hip shake. I imagine the rest of the neighbours in this cul-de-sac doing a little hip shaking, too, as the music wafts over the high metal gate, past the poster of the twenty most wanted men in the Philippines, the stray dogs sleeping in the sun, the men working in the cement factory up the street.

Two young teachers are holding up two boys with cerebral palsy. Another teacher redirects the teenagers, trying to keep them from yelling and biting or hitting themselves. Teacher Ruby is in the back with Joa and the other "big boys," men in their twenties and thirties, trying to get them to imitate Aubrey.

Karen Carpenter is followed by a scratchy version of the Philippine national anthem. I stand at attention with my hand over my heart, as the other teachers do. Aubrey leads the recitation of the Lord's Prayer, followed by the sign of the cross—the Father, the Son, and the Holy Ghost. Which I copy, furtively, unsure on which side the Holy Ghost resides. Then the kids file into the entrance of the old house, past the kitchen, up the stairs, their shoes scraping over the faded yellow linoleum.

I'm a speech-language pathologist on a volunteer assignment at this special needs school in Cebu City, Philippines. The students here have a variety of diagnoses—autism, cerebral palsy, developmental delay, Down syndrome. Half of them don't speak. Many have severe behaviour problems. Carol, the principal, wants programs for all the students, training for all the teachers, recommendations for the whole school. I have just three weeks here.

It takes me one week to get the kids sorted out—the classes, the names of the teachers and *titas* (assistants), and where the heck the "big boys" disappear to every morning. Children's birthdays are celebrated regularly. A teacher or *tita* tracks me down, invites me to come to the gym for a "happy meal," or brings me a piece of cake. The school is filled with music, the teachers are always singing.

The ladies of the school's parent foundation invite me to lunch at the Casino Español, a country club with Spanish-style turrets, courtyards, and a pool filled with noisy expat children splashing water and privilege.

When Carol and I arrive, the ladies are waiting. They chat in Visayan and English. Someone is presented with a birthday present: thong underwear. Someone asks me if I'm married. When I say no, they say I'm lucky not to have a man to tell me what to do. Do I like Filipino men? "Well, I don't know many, but the ones I've met seem nice," I say. "They are wonderful lovers," a lady says. "But not such good husbands," another remarks. Annie volunteers to find me one—for fun only, she says. I laugh and say something vague.

Of all the parents, I feel closest to Annie. She's told me how her son, Joa, keeps her up nights singing the national anthem. He once threw all the deck chairs over the side of a ferry. "I just closed my eyes for two minutes and when I opened them, the chairs were gone." She looks after her dad's and the school's finances, her three sons, and her husband. I like her sly, ironic sense of humour, the fact that she's the same size as I am and we can commiserate about not being able to fit into what passes for a large in the Philippines.

I start my day observing children in the classroom or during snack time, taking the ones who can co-operate enough to the library for assessments. I go up and down the stairs of this big house, trying to find kids. Often, they're not in their classrooms. Do they ever do schoolwork? How am I going to make my recommendations without seeing how they communicate in class? I have so little time.

Some of the children are learning sign language, but many don't have any way to communicate. The teachers, *titas*, the parents, the whole school could benefit from training in a specialized picture communication system, but the course costs five hundred dollars per person and is not available in Cebu.

At lunch, I make myself a coffee and go into the quiet treed yard off the kitchen for a break. Andre, a boy with Down syndrome, sits with me. He has a million questions. "You have animals in your country? What kind? Rats?" he asks, pointing to a giant one emerging from under the school. "You have monkeys? Water buffalo? Tigers? Lions?" Joa rocks back and forth on a swing opposite us, saying "Coffee, coffee." I smile and say, "Yes, coffee. My coffee." But it's not a comment he's making. He wants my coffee. He starts yelling and biting his hand. I've told the teachers to respond to all appropriate communication attempts. I know this is not appropriate but I'm tired and I don't want an episode: I give him the coffee.

We are going to the beach house of Mam Betty, the school's owner, for the weekend, at Catmon, north of the city. This excursion has been arranged by Carol, Annie, and Mam Betty because I expressed interest in travelling to another island and they don't want me to go on my own. The dangers: typhoons, overcrowded boats, Communist rebels, sweet-talking but unreliable Filipino men? So we are going to Catmon. Annie has convinced her husband to let her go. She's bringing her two younger boys, a self-contained twelve-year-old and seven-year-old David who calls me "the white lady." Carol is bringing her granddaughters. We were supposed to go this morning after my lecture on speech and language development. But the lecture started late. Then Annie and Carol took me to lunch at the Casino Español. Then we drove to Carol's to get the girls, then we waited for Mam Betty and her driver, for Annie and her kids. Then Carol had to buy diapers. Then she had to change the toddler's diaper.

We arrive at the beach house after dark. The kids bathe in a small pool and I go down to the rocky shore and watch the lights of night fishermen twinkle in the bay.

The next day, Mam Betty's driver comes for us in the early afternoon. David refuses to leave the pool where he's been playing with the other kids all morning, and throws an awe-inspiring tantrum.

At first, Annie thought that David was autistic, like Joa. He didn't speak until he was five. He has problems with grammar, vocabulary, and sentence structure. Can I assess him? Though he doesn't attend the school, and I doubt I can get to all of the kids there, I say yes. Annie has been kind to me, her life is hard, she's doing the best she can for her family. I think of the young Annie who won a scholarship to study in Cebu City, who was chosen to go to California on a Rotary Exchange. The young woman with a master's degree and a university teaching job she had to leave after she had Joa.

Carol weaves her truck in and out of dense traffic, honking her horn if a car lingers at a green light for more than a nanosecond. We're going to the "Colours of Hope" student art display and sale at the Ayala Mall. The proceeds are going to Special Olympics Philippines. Tonight is opening night.

I view the students' art with Carol and Alily, another foundation parent. She proudly tells me one of her daughter's drawings was reproduced on the bookmarks made for this event.

Carol scoots me to a seat then goes to the podium to lead the singing of the national anthem. There are prayers then speeches by local dignitaries. There is food. I lose Carol in the crowd. Annie tells me people have been praising Joa's picture. Alily steers me again to her daughter's picture and I think, I have only room in my luggage for one of them. But which one? I decide on Joa's piece, a hot air balloon in bright pink, orange, blue, with a tiny basket below. I can imagine him creating it, obsessively rolling the tiny pieces of coloured tissue paper into little balls, gluing them onto the paper pattern.

When Carol tells Annie I've bought Joa's picture, she hugs me and cries.

The last week I can't find kids to assess. They're late, they're rehearsing the Christmas play in the gym, they're in the courtyard, they're having snack, they're practising Christmas songs in someone else's classroom.

The karaoke machine has been moved to the entrance foyer and in the morning, at lunch, after school, the teachers gather around it, singing "Frosty the Snowman" and "Let It Snow." It is forty degrees in the shade here.

I am invited to a tribute to Janice, Mam Betty's daughter who had Down syndrome, who died last year. The teachers have prepared a slide show: Janice at a summer camp with the "big boys," Janice playing in the ocean, Janice smiling at the camera, Janice with her arm around Joa. The gym is packed with parents, students and teachers. After the slide show and speeches, some of the kids perform a dance to "One Way Ticket to the Blues." Then the teachers take to the stage, Aubrey leading them in a funny bump and grind routine to Abba's "Gimme! Gimme! Gimme! A Man after Midnight." One of Janice's favourite songs, apparently.

After lunch, the teachers and foundation members gather in the cemetery at Janice's crypt, a small white temple with her coffin on a raised dais in the centre. There a priest is waiting, despite the fact that Mam Betty's family is Protestant. "The teachers wanted a Catholic ceremony," she whispers to me. "I don't mind."

Later, Carol tells me that the "big boys" had tears in their eyes while watching the slide show. "They remember her," she says. "They can feel."

Today is the Christmas pageant. On the library computer, I work on my therapy recommendations, peeking out the door once in a while to see what's going on. Children, their faces painted with makeup and wearing their costumes over their green uniforms, sit quietly in groups.

Parents start arriving. There is a hum of activity outside my door. I follow it to the gym, where chairs have been set up in front of the stage. Seventies pop hits play over the sound system, parents fiddle with video cameras, siblings run up and down the aisles, the performers peek out from behind the curtains. The music stops, lights dim. The pageant begins.

I imagined the obligatory manger scene. And it's there, a beaming Mary with a doll for the baby Jesus surrounded by shepherds, the "big boys" dressed as wise men behind.

The curtains close then open and there are these scenes:

A poor mother brings her dying son to the hospital. She can't afford to pay. She begs the doctors to treat him. The doctors argue, one saying they can't admit him, the other saying they must. The scene ends with the compassionate doctor taking the boy to his private clinic, where he will treat him for free.

A rich and arrogant lawyer in a shiny white shirt finds himself in a street with many beggars. He is bumped, his briefcase falls. Will it be stolen? No, a beggar recovers the briefcase and returns it to the lawyer. The lawyer hugs the beggars.

The kids are brilliant. They use pantomime, gestures, and movement so well that the explanatory voice-over is unnecessary. The ones who are not acting sit quietly in front of the stage. Nobody yells or scratches or bites or hits. I'd wondered about the amount of time being spent in rehearsals, the time where the kids sat waiting to practise. Time that could be better spent in the classroom, I thought.

Now I see what the teachers have been doing.

After the pageant, Carol calls me to the stage to thank me for my work She gives me a card, handmade by Aubrey: three orange candles with silver flames. Inside is a prayer, which the audience sings to me:

> May your troubles all be small ones,
> And your fortune ten times ten.
> May the good Lord bless and keep you
> Till we meet again.

I stand outside the Cebu ferry terminal in the sweltering heat waiting for Annie and her driver to pick me up. They arrive, finally, Annie apologizing for being late, saying she had to pick something up. She asks about my trip (which she arranged) and I sing the praises of the Chocolate Hills and beaches of Bohol. At the condo where I'm staying, she opens the trunk. Inside is a guitar, from one of the factories on Mactan Island. The "thing" she had to pick up. "It's a present from the foundation," she says. "To thank you. So you won't forget us."

She remembered what I had forgotten. How, soon after I arrived, I said I'd heard they made beautiful guitars on Mactan. She'd asked me if I played and I said yes, I'd once studied the guitar but I hadn't played in years.

IT IS MINUS TEN, an unseasonably warm day for Edmonton in December. I unzip my new guitar from its soft black case. I was not allowed to bring it on the plane as carry-on and I fully expect the neck to be broken, the wood to be cracked and splintered after four flights. Remarkably, it has survived unscathed in its cardboard container. I should have had more faith in Annie. She said it wouldn't break.

The guitar is varnished a rich, golden colour, the strings are close to the fret and easy to hold down. I pick it up and tune each string. And then I begin to play.

MERIENDA

(snack)

CHAMPAGNE POWDER

I'VE LOST BARRY. He and his bright orange boots have vanished into the white void below. All alone on this black-diamond run, I curse myself for not studying the map, for letting my friend plan our day. I pick my way down a steep pitch, plowing through heavy snow, then slam into a mogul and fall hard on my right shoulder. Where the hell is Barry? He knows I've never skied here before. Why isn't he waiting, I think, hauling myself up. But he is waiting at the chairlift, waving and yelling from the lift line.

I have been downhill skiing since I was twelve. In the 1980s, I skied at Sunshine or Lake Louise most weekends. In the nineties, I managed a day once or twice a month. Now, most of my friends having stopped skiing—it is too expensive, or too hard on their bodies. Or because of the snowboarding hordes swooping down on skiers like twentieth-century Mongols, scraping off the good snow. Only Bar and I are left. We both have arthritic joints, his worse than mine. Two years ago, I tore the meniscus in my knee and have only managed a handful of ski days since. But I've agreed to drive to Colorado with Barry, where he's researching ski hills for a newspaper article. He promised good roads, sun, spring skiing. We'd ski rare champagne powder: snow that starts as rain from the

Pacific, has water sucked from it over the mountains so it is dry, light, fluffy. Powder that tickles your nose like champagne bubbles. He also promised I'd be back in time for my sisters reunion in Victoria in April.

I said yes. Because thirty-six years after I first put on a pair of neon yellow K2s, I have yet to ski the thing for which all skiers yearn: powder up to one's knees, thighs. The smooth, dry champagne powder for which Colorado, with elevations over twelve thousand feet, is famous.

And I still love speeding down hills. When I am skiing well, the universe falls into place. My knees don't ache. My quads don't burn. My body sheds years like unwanted pounds.

So, on a grey March day, I pick up Barry in my little Kia and we head south from Calgary, Barry munching on egg salad sandwiches, bits of egg falling onto his lap, as I pass semis on Highway 2. I have known Barry for twenty-five years. We put up with each other's idiosyncrasies: a desire to eat messy sandwiches while driving (his); an insistence that one be able to see half a kilometre down the road before attempting to pass (mine); a belief that there is no need to pay more than forty dollars a night for accommodation (his); a conviction that even the tiniest of small towns has a coffee shop that can make a decent latte (mine). Yes, a pair of eccentrics.

Barry grew up an army brat in England, Germany, and Canada, moving every couple of years. I grew up in Williams Lake and Kamloops. His family vacations consisted of driving to distant destinations, staying a day or two, then driving back. Mine involved going to our cabin at Chimney Lake, swimming, canoeing, and bird watching. He likes to drive. I don't. He does extensive research and route planning. I read novels about the place.

Yet we adore the same books, movies, art. And without Bar, how would I get my pop culture fix? Where would I learn about British comedies: *I'm Alan Partridge*, *Blackadder*, *Absolutely Fabulous*, and *Little Britain*? Who would keep me amused on long road trips by reading aloud books by David Sedaris, Jon Lee Anderson, Paul William Roberts. Bios of Ronnie Spector and the Pet Shop Boys. A history of Joy Division.

We are always looking for that perfect something: book, painting, piece of music. But as siblings and malcontents will do, we can drive each other crazy. Like when he tries to wrestle out of his coat while driving and takes his hands off the wheel. Like when I take everything out of my suitcase and sprawl clothes around the room, looking for that T-shirt I am sure I brought.

My parents always wanted a boy. We four girls wanted a baby brother. A baby boy we could dress up, boss around, show off. We had "pseudo-brothers": my parents' friends' son Kimmy, whose idea of fun was to tie us up with our own skipping ropes. Dad hired the occasional fatherless teenage boy to mow the lawn, shovel snow, build a retaining wall. But we girls did that kind of work too.

A music-loving hippie kid living in military housing in the fifties and sixties, Barry didn't have to do much "boy work." I've helped him do things like put up a shower curtain or screw legs onto a coffee table. If he were my brother, Dad would have whipped him into shape.

While we wanted a brother, Barry had one who died. He rarely mentions him, and respecting his privacy, I don't ask.

Fourteen driving hours and one night in Twin Falls, Idaho, later, we are in Wyoming. The light is flat and wind whistles snow across Highway 30, polishing it to an icy sheen. My shoulders are aching from clutching the wheel.

"Rock Springs coming up," says Bar, looking up from the map.

"As in the book."

"Mm-hmm."

I stare at trailers strewn across the side of a hill and think about Richard Ford's characters. Ranchers down on their luck, small boys betrayed by their parents' lust, realtors and drinkers, eccentrics and misfits. Dreamers. Characters living in this hard-scrabble landscape, or en route to a place of better fortune.

Steamboat Springs is still hours away. We are the only vehicle on a narrow stretch of black macadam leading to Craig, Colorado. The desert falls away on either side. There's little vegetation to stop the howling wind and blowing snow. We ride on a black tunnel of tarmac, wind rattling the windows and buffeting my car. The snow turns to ice and freezes on the wiper blades and headlights, leaving me only a small circle of vision. Past Craig, there are a few more vehicles, mostly trucks and SUVs with chains. We have no chains. Finally, twelve hours after setting out, we reach the deserted main street of Steamboat.

"Spring, huh?" I grunt, unfolding my stiff body in the motel parking lot.

"Springtime in the Rockies," he declares. "Where the elusive champagne powder awaits."

The all-you-can-eat breakfast buffet at the Rabbit Ears Motel features dry Wonder bread, rubbery boiled eggs, and overripe bananas. Barry happily chows down. I tell him there is an organic coffee shop and bakery just down the street. "No time. If we want to ski powder, we have to be on the hill when the lifts open. It'll be gone by noon." I finish the brown water that is apparently coffee and follow him out the door to wait for the ski bus.

Barry agrees to do the wide, mogul-free blue or easy black runs I prefer, and I consent to a couple of double blacks, where my only goal is to stay upright. He tells me I am turning too much ("That is how I learned"). I tell him he is going too fast ("Well, that's how I learned"). It's a good though powderless day. I was nervous, given that I'd only been on skis a couple of times this winter, but I did all right. Even got in a few runs where my rhythm was smooth and the turns felt effortless.

That night after six straight hours on the slopes, we lie sore and exhausted in our beds, watching TV.

"Change the channel," I say. "Let's see how much more snow we're in for."

"How does this remote thing work?"

"I dunno, press the arrows."

"I don't see any arrows."

"There should be a button with silver triangles."

"Where?"

"Oh, for God's sake, throw it here!"

I could call Barry a Luddite, but that doesn't describe him because I can't imagine him destroying machinery, other than accidentally crashing his computer by pushing *enter* too many times.

We drive to Vail. Haul our gear from our hotel through this faux-Swiss village to the lift line. The queue chatter is about the seventeen inches of snow that has fallen in the night. There are fewer wool-clad telemarkers here than at

Steamboat, more folks in designer ski suits. I glance down at my ensemble: faded blue Gore-Tex jacket and black snow pants, just slightly more stylish than Barry's dirty red bomber jacket and torn blue wind pants.

"Wow, I haven't seen those skis since the eighties," a guy with skis parabola-ed for powder says to Barry.

"They're from the nineties," he protests.

The guy raises an eyebrow. "Yeah? Well, good luck on them."

"He's a great skier," I say in sisterly defence. Barry beams.

We start with a few intermediate runs, the blues, then move on to the blacks, Barry ahead, me pushing myself to keep up.

"My quads are mush," I say after a few hours.

"You're holding your edge too long. Let your skis run and your legs won't get so sore."

Bar learned to ski in Germany, where I imagine they put you on very long skis then a gondola to the top of some forty-five degree piste, and said, "*Folge mir.*" Follow me. I learned to ski at Kamloops's Harper Mountain, a family-run hill where the gentle Swiss instructors used the graduated length method, starting you on short skis and gradually increasing them. A perfect method for people who don't like to lose control.

Garfinkel's is the cheap family restaurant we've compromised on because I wanted dinner out and Barry thought we could dine in on his stock of tuna sandwiches from Calgary. A group of young men treat our section of the restaurant as their personal party room, yelling crudely at each other and braying at the waitresses for more beer. Computer-generated snowboarders do tricks on multiple TVs. Metal blasts from nearby speakers. I ask Barry about skiing in Switzerland in the seventies. Could you really schuss from village to village, from one cozy chalet lodge to the next? Did he and the other skiers share a communal table eating spätzle and schnitzel, toasting each other with schnapps, before falling into a dreamless eiderdown sleep?

"Kinda," he replies, "though there was more Stella than schnapps."

Although he is ten years older, I imagine myself his younger sister, trailing after him there. Trying to keep up.

We wander home. I am ready for bed but Barry wants to go to the outdoor hot tub in the hotel's courtyard because it is included in the room price. It is snowing lightly, the sky dancing with stars, the tub empty. Music wafts from hidden stereo speakers. I recognize a few songs, Elvis singing "Kentucky Rain," Barry Manilow's "I Write the Songs," but Bar knows them all: "Tower of Strength," "Baby Workout," "Sealed with a Kiss," one of his favourites. I can picture young Barry sending a letter to some exotic beauty, some utterly unattainable object of desire. If I'd known him in his youth, I would have warned him, given him some sisterly advice. That kind of champagne-powder girl is high maintenance, Bar. That kind of girl will break your heart.

In Aspen, we stay at the Limelight Lodge, a hotel that Barry visited with his mom several years ago. Refurbished after a fire, it features high ceilings, a stone fireplace, blond wood, steel appliances, and king-sized beds.

"Wow, this is nice."

"Liked it better before," grumbles Bar, sniffling and clearing his throat. "It was comfier. Homier."

"Are you getting sick?"

"Maybe."

"What kind of sick?"

"A cold."

"You better not give it to me. I've got my sisters weekend coming up, remember," I say, placing hand sanitizer on his night table.

The next day, he's coughing more.

"You look pale. Better stay in bed."

"I'm skiing."

"Don't be ridiculous."

"I have to write my article."

"I'll take notes for you."

"You won't ski the blacks without me."

"I will," I say. I won't.

"Liar."

The following day, Barry's face is grey, his eyes bloodshot, his cough deep and phlegmy. I am getting worried.

"You look terrible. I'm buying you some cough syrup."

"I'm okay."

"You're not. You hack every two minutes. And you should drink more water, you're probably getting dehydrated. There is no way you can ski today."

"I have to review Snowmass for the article."

"I told you, I'll ski all the runs, I'll take notes."

"I'm coming."

"Martyr."

We ski the first run at Snowmass in a whiteout. For the first time I'm out front, stopping regularly to wait for Barry. Then he falls, something I've never seen him do before.

"What happened?" I ask at the lift lineup.

"I don't know. I can't turn any more for some reason."

"You're too sick to be out here."

"Maybe, but I have a story to write."

His tenacity is appealing. That and his sense of humour are what made me like him in the first place. I remember a back-country ski trip to Dolomite Pass in the Rockies, where we skinned up and he plodded up the mountain on ancient splintered wooden skis, celebrating by pulling a glass bottle of beer from his pack, downing it while doing the chicken dance. Maybe he doesn't feel pain. Maybe he thinks ignoring or denying pain will make it disappear. I can be the same, pushing my body beyond what it wants to do. We aren't that young any more, I want to tell him. Our bodies don't bounce back, no matter how much we wish they would.

"You need a break, Bar. Please. I mean, I'm tired. I'd like a break."

"Okay," he says, and we clomp inside the lodge for a coffee, which he sips between coughing fits.

"Let's go to a clinic. Or hospital. Just to get you checked out."

"I don't have medical insurance."

Of course he doesn't have medical insurance.

That evening, Barry is asleep by six, medicine and tissues strewn around his bed. The room has a sour, yeasty smell. We need to get back to Canada. Tomorrow.

Highway 70 to Denver is lousy with potholes. Pickup trucks, SUVs, and semis fly by in the passing lane. Snow blows across the tarmac, black ice shines where canyon walls shade the road. At Denver, we head north to the Wyoming border. Highway 25 was closed yesterday because of a heavy snowfall, and now semi after semi passes us, streaming south. I stop because Bar wants to drive, but he is hacking so much that I soon make him pull over and commandeer the wheel.

I drive as fast as feels safe through a wide Wyoming plain, round, snow-capped mountains on the horizon. Drifts dance across the highway. The road is empty of cars now, and as Barry dozes, I think how easy it would be to get caught in a snowstorm here, to turn down the wrong road, to be snowed in, like characters in an Annie Dillard story. It is lonely country to be travelling with a sick friend whose face is now more blue than grey.

At the Sheridan Super 8, we take separate rooms so his coughing doesn't keep me up, so I can get enough sleep to drive the rest of the way home.

I bring him a hamburger and iced tea.

"I can't eat."

"At least drink something," I say. "You're definitely dehydrated."

"I'm not thirsty."

I open the bottle. "Here," I say. He takes a few swallows.

I get up in the night, wander down the hall, and knock on his door. Nothing. I knock louder. Again. And again.

Then I hear the cough. Thank God. He's alive.

In Calgary, Barry goes to the hospital, is diagnosed with a throat abscess and dehydration and put on IV fluids. I do not get a throat abscess. It turns out they are not contagious. In Victoria for my sisters reunion, I admire the red and yellow tulips waving their pretty heads, the cherry trees full of snowy pink blossoms. The grass is green, the air warm and lilac-scented. It's hard to believe in winter here.

Barry and I did ski champagne powder back on the second day of our trip. Pushed off down the pristine slope under a cornflower sky, skiing side by side for once. I let my skis run.

A cloud of snow hovered about my knees. I felt light, buoyant, as if I were floating.

This, I thought, is why we suffer through the white-knuckle drives to the mountains, the long lineups, the gangs of snowboarders, the aches and pains. This is what we are looking for, my bro and I. The few minutes where our minds shut down and we are only our strong and beautiful bodies, dancing.

ON SHYNESS AND STUTTERING

> *"The legitimacy of my voice, wherever I am, seems a question. In New York and then New England, I have been surrounded by people who do not talk quite as I do. I tend, like a foreigner, to resist dropping consonants . . . I pronounce words as they look in print . . . Yet we all, in a world of mingling clans, exist in some form of linguistic exile, and most people don't stutter."*
>
> —John Updike, "Getting the Words Out," *Self-Consciousness*

WHEN I WAS NINETEEN, I left my small British Columbia town to attend the University of Victoria. I moved into residence, a co-ed hall, where there were alternating floors of boys and girls. My roommate, Avril, was a solid, lumberjack-shirt-wearing girl with a punk haircut and a brusque manner. She was studying Russian, and her side of the slab of wood that ran across the end of the room by the window and was our desk was always piled with weighty tomes. She wasn't in the room much. She didn't talk to me much.

I remember sitting at the desk with my transistor radio tuned to CFOX, reading *Candide* or *La Peste* or *Le Malade Imaginaire,* my French-English dictionary beside me, the laughter of my floormates "studying" in the lounge echoing down the hallway. I'd done well in my classes in my first year at Cariboo College, even won the French essay prize (Racine's collected works) for an essay I wrote, the subject of which I can't recall (was it on Sartre's *No Exit*?). In Kamloops, I spent weekends writing English essays with titles like "Symbolic Naturalism in Ibsen's *The Wild Duck,*" and "The Human Predicament as Dramatized in Samuel Beckett's *Endgame,*" burnishing sentences for my velvet-suited hippy English prof on whom I had a crush.

Late one night as I was polishing a French essay, Avril came into our room. She asked me a question. I can't remember what the question was. I can't remember what I answered, but I clearly recall her saying, in a scornful voice, "Why are you always stuttering?"

I've always been shy, but I didn't and don't consider myself a person who stutters. Though, when I was younger, I often had the sensation of tightness in my chest, of squeezing out the last words of a sentence. These breathing problems happened when I had to read aloud, answer a question in class, and especially when I had to give a presentation.

I'd been willing to venture the odd comment in my college classes in Kamloops, but I didn't talk at UVic, where I was studying English, creative writing, and French. I was intimidated by the fluency of my fellow French conversation class students, many of whom had been in French Immersion or had spent summers in Quebec.

I had been looking forward to taking a fiction-writing class with Audrey Thomas because as a twelve-year-old, I'd taken summer camp with her. She'd liked my stories then. She'd said I wrote good dialogue. But I was one of the youngest in her class, so I sat silently, listening to the older, worldlier students explain their motivations and themes (in case we'd missed them). They wrote about drug-addiction, death, and divorce. You were supposed to "write what you know," and I didn't know about any of those things. I can't remember what I wrote about. Childhood, maybe? I do remember going to an end-of-the-year party at Audrey's apartment. I sat silently at the edge of the group, a classic example of Joseph Sheehan's "approach-avoidance" theory of stuttering (both wanting to talk and not wanting to talk in equal measure), wondering how long I had to stay, and when I could leave without being rude.

"I still feel Elizabeth needs much encouragement to give her a true feeling of confidence in her own abilities. She has done delightful and original work. I think she may always find it hard to have confidence in her own abilities," wrote a former teacher on my report card. My prescient kindergarten teacher. She went on to say I might have trouble with transition to grade one but that "a sympathetic teacher recognizing [her] ability should be able to help her overcome this."

I apparently made the transition to grade one well. I liked school. My teacher recommended that I skip grade two, but at the end of the year we moved to Vancouver. In Vancouver, it turned out I wasn't to skip a grade. In fact, I was enrolled in a special remedial arithmetic class which involving learning to count by fives and tens with blue- and orange-coloured rods and cones, something all Vancouver children mastered by the end of grade one, evidently. And though I was crazy about reading and books, I was acutely aware of being in only the "second highest" reading group there.

I had a babysitter I loved, though, who taught me French. She made me a book with magazine pictures carefully labelled *en français*. I practised saying those words over and over.

At the end of grade two, we moved to Kamloops. Encouraged by my grade three and four teachers, and my mom, I started writing stories. Mom subscribed to the Saskatchewan newspaper of her childhood, *The Western Producer*, which featured a children's creative writing section. I regularly contributed stories to it under the pen name Kami, our town's rainbow trout mascot.

At home, I played with my younger sisters and the neighbourhood kids, but I would also often sneak off to find a quiet place to read and write. When I was nine, we went to Gabriola Island for our summer vacation. I found a big, hollowed-out rock on the beach, which I could line with towels and pillows to make a cozy nook. Paradise, I thought; no pesky younger sisters to bother me, and a stack of fresh Nancy Drews to read. When we visited my aunt, uncle, and seven cousins in their old stone house in Prescott, Ontario, I discovered many of the rooms had window seats, which could be lined with pillows and blankets. If I pulled the velvet curtains closed and was very quiet, I could read and write for hours, undisturbed.

After my year at UVic, I transferred to Western Washington University in Bellingham to study Speech-Language Pathology. This was my dad's idea. He thought I could combine my love of words and languages with a profession that would allow me to "make a decent living." I rejected his other ideas—high school English or French teacher—out of hand. Teachers had to speak in front of people, whole classes of hormone-crazed teenagers. I could barely talk to one person at a time. And though I secretly wanted to be a journalist, I didn't think I'd be able to interview strangers, especially strangers who had just been in a car accident or were injured or in pain. I also wanted to be a novelist but knew, from what my dad said, that down that path lay penury.

Dad arranged for me to talk to a local speech pathologist. She said I could work with kids or adults, in a school or hospital. I enjoyed kids, one on one, and I didn't mind hospitals. But although I liked my classes at Western Washington, I quickly discovered I was an introvert in classrooms full of extroverts. Did my classmates ever stop talking? I went from school to my small room in a boarding house, where, during the week, I stayed up until the early hours studying so I could drive to Vancouver on the weekends to see my boyfriend. The house was full of eccentrics: Dale, a violin maker who had long red hair which he either wore long or piled high on his head like a debutante and lived in the attic; Les, a cross-dressing music student who borrowed my clothes; "Disco Martin," who worked in a fish-canning plant, arriving home every night at 2 a.m. and cranking Donna Summer; Kim, who insisted that Prince Charles would marry a Korean girl, most likely her. I felt comfortable in my rambling house of misfits, more than with my fellow speech pathology students.

I worked for a year, then went to Washington State University for my master's degree. The speech pathology graduate program at WSU was small, the profs friendly and helpful. They went to the pub with us. They knew our names. In fact, Elizabeth was deemed too "formal," so I was known by my childhood nickname of E.J. there. I was one of several Canadians in the program, the department head having a fondness for Canadian students, who, he maintained, kept the departmental GPA high. Though I still felt shy inside, I'd learned that my profs would listen when I talked, and the more I spoke in class, the more comfortable I became answering questions and offering my opinion.

When I was in my early thirties and working, someone gave me a book about the Myers-Briggs personality inventory. I read it. I did the test. I had a eureka moment. Here was an explanation for my feelings of being different from other people, of needing to spend time on my own. I *was* different from most other people. I was an INFJ, the personality type of about 1 percent of the population. According to www.mypersonality.info, INFJ's are "artistic and creative," "live in a world of hidden meanings," focus on fantasy more than reality (hmm, an evening with the new Michael Ondaatje novel, or a party, what's to choose?), fear doing the wrong thing (yup), are observers (uh-huh) and avoiders (you bet), sensitive, tend to be devoted to what they believe in (there is a reason my boyfriends were of the leftist, placard-bearing kind). Many of my good friends turned out to be INFPs, another rare and similar type.

Speech pathology was not listed as a career suggestion for INFJs, though writer was. Yet my dad was right. I've enjoyed speech-language pathology, and it has provided me with an interesting way to make a living. Almost accidentally, I ended up specializing in the treatment of stuttering. In grad school, I was assigned to be the research assistant of Dr. Marcel Wingate, a theorist and researcher whose standard definition of stuttering is still widely used. My first job was at the Calgary General Hospital, where I was hired because they needed someone to run the outpatient stuttering program and no one on staff wanted to do it.

I found my adult stuttering clients to be a compelling and diverse group. I met people who, like John Updike, went to considerable efforts to hide their speech problem. I met people who didn't. I met introverts and extroverts. I met clients who said they'd be extroverts if talking wasn't so difficult, and who indeed became more extroverted as their fluency improved.

I got involved with a rather militant American self-help organization called the National Stuttering Project (they protested Michael Palin's portrayal of stuttering in the movie *A Fish Called Wanda*, Porky Pig, and other negative depictions of stuttering in the media). I learned how stuttering and people's negative reactions to it could shape and silence a person. I read the actor James Earl Jones's autobiography, *Voices and Silences*. Because of his stutter, Jones was essentially mute and didn't speak from the ages of six to fourteen—didn't speak, that is, until an English professor challenged him to prove he hadn't plagiarized a poem he wrote by reading it aloud. Jones did so and discovered he had an actor's voice: deep and rich and resonant.

I moved to a job in public health but continued to specialize in treating stuttering. I helped the local support group, and we organized a national conference for people who stutter, called "Many Paths, One Journey." In 2002, I joined the staff at the Institute for Stuttering Treatment and Research.

What has kept me working in this area is the courage of my clients. The six-year-old boy who told me he would be more curious if he didn't stutter. The thirteen-year-old who, tired of enduring the gossipy bullying of other teenage girls which didn't change after she told her teachers, asked her mom to get her out of that school and find her some speech therapy. The fifty-year-old who, fed up with having some of his fellow ESL students giggle, roll their eyes, or look impatient when he spoke, stood up, wrote "stuttering" on the whiteboard, and proceeded to explain to the class what it was and why it was so difficult for him to talk. He asked for their patience. He asked for their respect and got it.

"I think a stutterer ends up with a greater need to express himself, or perhaps, a greater awareness of the deep human need for expression," writes James Earl Jones in his 1993 book *Voices and Silences*. Being a stutterer, he continues, "leaves you painfully aware of how you would like to say something. And I would know, as an afterthought, how I could have said this or that. But at the moment you are too busy making the choice to speak or not to speak, to use this word or that word. The pain is in the reflection. The desire to speak builds and builds until it becomes part of your energy; your life force . . . When I was a boy, speech became a wall I could not surmount."

I have come to realize what a complex problem stuttering is. Neurophysiology, genetics, learning, and environment all play a part. I have seen how deeply stuttering can affect people. I meet parents who feel tremendous guilt about their children's stuttering, who cry with relief when I tell them that they didn't cause the problem. I meet very young children who, within a week of starting to stutter, covered their mouths and said, "Mommy, help me talk." I meet adults who, bullied as children, have gone underground, who won't mention or discuss their stuttering with anyone, not even their spouse.

Contrary to what we may see in movies like *A Fish Called Wanda*, there is no single "stuttering personality." Though the stereotype is that people who stutter are shy, timid, nervous, and lacking in confidence, studies have shown they are, as a group, no more likely to be maladjusted than people who don't stutter, though they may, understandably, have more fears about speaking. That so many of my clients are willing to work hard to overcome those fears is testament to their strength and courage, in a society that still doesn't quite understand stuttering.

Sometimes my clients tell me that they want to speak perfectly, like "normal speakers." I understand the sentiment (if only I could write perfectly, like this or that author), but tell them that no one has perfect fluency. We all repeat, revise, say *um* and *ah*, hem and haw. I tell them perfect fluency can sound memorized, glib, and insincere, like the speech of a famous scientist I once heard whose rapid speech rate and hyperfluency made it difficult to absorb anything he was saying. I agree with John Updike, whose 1989 memoir *Self-Consciousness* argued that "people who talk too easily and comfortably, with too much happy rolling of the vowels and satisfied curling of the lips around the grammatical rhythms, rouse distrust in some atavistic, pre-speech part of ourselves; we turn off. Whereas those who stutter win, in the painful pauses of their demonstration that speech isn't entirely natural, a respectful attention, a tender alertness. Words are, we are reassured, precious."

Indeed they are. Nowadays, people often express surprise when I tell them I am shy (though, as a shy person, I don't do this routinely!). "You don't seem shy," they say. And it's true. I rarely blush any more when strangers talk to me. I can make good eye contact. These are things that I've learned. I've watched outgoing people and copied them. I've made myself enter situations I'd prefer to avoid (cocktail parties with rich, well-dressed people; actually, cocktail parties with anyone). I've joined Toastmasters. Still, in a group, I'm drawn to the people who hang back. The people who don't immediately overwhelm with you with talk but who may, if they sense you are sincerely interested in them, offer a thoughtful comment or two.

In a society that values extroverts, I suggest we pay more attention to the introverts (though not in a showy way that calls undue attention to them, God, please!). The quiet girl who watches her peers, then silently joins their play, showing them a better way to make that paper boat float. The boy at the back of the class, drawing and writing in his notebook. Observe them. Find out what they're good at. They might be architects, artists, writers. Be assured, they are watching, thinking, observing. There are fascinating things happening in their heads that we'll never know about unless we take the time to ask. Unless we take the time to listen.

CENA

(dinner)

LEAVING LARES

FIVE O'CLOCK IN THE MORNING. In silence, my sister Leslie and I shiver into layers of polypro and fleece then carry our packs down the red-carpeted steps of the Posada del Corregidor. Lorenzo, the guide we hired privately after he impressed us on an organized trip to Machu Picchu, waits in a taxi. We glide down the dawn streets of Cuzco, Peru, past the dark *catedral*, a Quechua woman setting up her blankets and sweaters on the sidewalk, narrow *calles* with looming Incan walls.

The bus to Calca is crowded. Windows slide open of their own accord as we squeal around corners. The passengers sit silent, the men in their ponchos and woollen earflapped toques, the women draped in boldly striped blankets. Lorenzo sits across from my sister and me in this cold, unheated bus. We huddle together, poring over the book *The Conquest of the Incas*. When one of us wants the page to be turned, she nods and the other paws the book with mittened hands. We read five hundred years into the past, about the last stand of Manco II, King of the Inca. He fought and almost beat the Spanish, was captured and escaped to Ollantaytambo in the Sacred Valley, to the northwest, which we are hurtling toward though it is not our destination.

At Calca, Lorenzo arranges a ride for us in a pickup truck going to Lares, farther north into the mountains. The narrow gravel road switchbacks as it climbs, each turn revealing more snow-covered peaks and sliding us from our bags of potatoes and onto nearby wriggling gunnysacks of guinea pigs headed for slaughter.

On the main street of Lares, beneath looming mountains and an overcast sky, children have gathered to perform a dance: boys in brilliant red-and-pink fringed ponchos and woollen hats, the girls with knee-length skirts and shawls, their hats like embroidered upside-down bowls. We joke that this welcoming committee is for us. Lorenzo laughs and tells us it is for education officials who are on a regular school inspection tour. We join the ring of onlookers. Beside me, a teenage girl tenderly braids a little one's hair. The younger one is still as the older girl combs and winds. Sisters, I wonder?

We watch the dancing and then we leave Lares. Lorenzo walks us along a bumpy road that becomes a small dirt track through the forest. Leslie marches ahead; Lorenzo and I follow.

"She is very strong," Lorenzo says to me in Spanish.

"Yes," I say. "She pushes her husband, Randy, in his wheelchair."

"Was he in an accident?"

"No, a disease. A degenerative neurological condition."

Lorenzo nods. In his eyes, a look of deep sorrow.

We hired Lorenzo for his kindness. As our guide the previous week on the trail to Machu Picchu, he'd helped each person in our group of twelve, where Leslie and I were known collectively as the Sisters. He'd gone back and forth along the path, assisting Les, whose ankles were threatening to collapse on the steep Incan steps down to Huiñay Huayna; leading an acrophobic trekker down a gully; and coming back to check on me, the oldest in our group, Señorita Isobel of the bad knees.

Lorenzo was born in Huayllabamba, the pueblo where we spent our first night en route to Machu Picchu. He grew up speaking Quechua. At eighteen, he left his village for Cuzco, where he worked as a servant and learned Spanish. He became a trekking porter, a cook, then a guide. He earns about twenty dollars for four days' work guiding gringos to Machu Picchu, making sure we don't sit on the ancient Incan walls or stray down the wrong valley, that we are fed and watered and healthy and warm. He lives with his ninety-five-year-old father and supports a large extended family.

"*Señorita Isobel, puedo preguntarte algo*?" he'd asked me as I dragged my carcass up Dead Woman's Pass, the highest point of the Inca Trail.

"*Si, como no*?" I'd answered in Spanish. Yes, why not?

"Where is your husband?"

"Good question."

"He ran away?"

"No, I'm single."

He asked if I lived with my parents or Leslie and Randy. I told him I lived alone.

THE DAY BEFORE Les flew in to Cuzco, I moved out of my basic one-star hotel and found us a big room in a comfy hotel on the central Plaza de Armas. I was eager to show Les what I'd seen, tell her what I knew. I was looking forward to being with her after four months of travelling through South and Central America alone.

But she arrived exhausted after working fourteen-hour days, trying to cope with the demands of a stressful job and her husband's disease. She'd flown in from sea level, and the altitude was making her sick.

She wanted us each to rent our own tent. I convinced her one tent was better—warmer, less weight, and less expense. I didn't say her idea made me sad. I am searching, I think, for a sister who doesn't want to be found. One I haven't lived with for twenty years. One I've made up. One who doesn't exist.

Several kilometres beyond Lares, we come to an Incan hot springs. Stone columns surround the square pool. Water flows down into it from spigots in the columns. Steam rises from the muddy surface. A rickety wooden change house sits off to one side. It has two stalls, half doors, and a concrete floor, just like the change house behind the house where Les and I grew up in Kamloops. Me, the oldest of four girls; Les, the baby, seven years younger. Let me rephrase that: where *I* grew up. When I was nineteen and Leslie was twelve, my family moved to Alabama. Les grew up, became a young woman, there; I stayed behind in Canada to finish university.

I called her baby, and brat. She found cigarettes in my bottom drawer, listened to my phone conversations about drinking parties, threatened to tell Mom. She had nightmares. Often, she'd appear at my door in the middle of the night, wanting to sleep with me. "No stealing the covers," I'd tell her. But the kid was always burning hot, and I ended up pushing the blankets she'd kicked off back onto her.

Leslie jumps into the hot pool, yelling, "Come in, it's beautiful."

I ease gooseflesh into steaming water.

"Lorenzo, *puedes tomar una foto de nosotros*?" I ask.

Les and I put our arms around each other. Water streams down the stone irrigation channels at our backs.

"Cheese," Lorenzo says.

"*Queso!*" we yell.

We follow a dirt path upwards, nothing but grey sky and green hills above us. A boy herding sheep offers a shy "*buenas tardes*." At Tamboallaua, we talk to some men who are roasting the potatoes they have been harvesting. The men offer us *chicha*, corn liquor. I take it but Leslie declines. Why? She accepts the grassy-tasting coca leaf tea Lorenzo offers for altitude sickness. I have been travelling longer, have been healthy, and am willing to take more risks. Maybe she is worried the *chicha* is made with something that will make her sick. Because Randy relies on her, she can't afford to get ill.

Passing cows and sheep, I climb alone into a cold fog. See my first llama. I take out my camera and creep closer, but when I am about three metres away, he bolts, only to stop again a metre or so ahead, looking back at me with enormous, lashed eyes. I follow him up to the village of Cuncani. Near the stone schoolhouse there, the teacher waylays Lorenzo, asking that we camp in the schoolyard, telling him it will be safer and the money we pay will help the school. Lorenzo refuses, telling us later the money will only get as far as the teacher's pocket. We will stay with Santiago, our porter.

Santiago's home is one narrow room built of stone. At one end is a fireplace where several children, from toddlers to adolescents, sit on a stone bench. Santiago's wife crouches over the fireplace, preparing dinner. Les and I sit at the other end on benches covered with llama skins, shivering despite our multiple layers of clothing and drinking coca tea. Smoke from the fire has blackened the walls. Guinea pigs run past our feet. Les and I exchange glances. "*Cuy*," says Lorenzo. I look at the furry brown-and-white animals skittering back and forth across the stones. "Very good, *muy sabroso*," he says when a little boy shyly offers us their legs on a platter. I think to tell Lorenzo that in Canada we keep them as pets, but don't. He may already know this. He may think it crazy.

Santiago, Lorenzo tells us, is "*muy fuerte*." Very strong. At forty-six, Santiago has eight children, the youngest just walking, the oldest married. The youngest huddle together, sending us shy glances.

"His wife gets up at two o'clock *en la madrugada*," Lorenzo says. She prepares Santiago's breakfast so he can be out tending his animals—sheep and llamas—by four.

According to my Spanish-English dictionary, *a quien madruga, Dios le ayuda* means "the early bird captures the worm," but the literal translation is "God helps those who rise early." I would like to believe this is true, but then I think of the small, malnourished children I've seen in Peru, their thin clothes and rubber sandals, their black or missing teeth. I think of Randy, my brother-in-law, whose disease causes such spasticity, such pain that he often can't sleep.

The next morning Lorenzo stays behind to pack. I follow Les who follows Santiago's son up a wandering path, past waterfalls and blue lakes dotted across a rocky meadow. We trudge up to a cold, windy pass 4,200 metres above sea level, behind this twelve-year-old boy who has the strength of a man, then we head down and up another small pass.

"How's your ankle?" I ask Les when I finally catch up to her.

"Fine," she says, though I can see the old injury is acting up again and she is limping.

I try to keep her in sight as we trail Santiago's son down the pass. Then Lorenzo is with us and the boy is gone.

Passing a pueblo with three stone houses, Lorenzo says he wishes that the parents wouldn't have so many children, that all the children could go to school. He speaks in Spanish, and I translate for Les.

"You don't need to translate," she says. "I understand a lot. I'll ask you when I don't."

I want to reply, testily, that I am just trying to help, but catch myself. Maybe she is grouchy because her ankle is hurting. A bit jealous because Lorenzo is talking to me more than her. Or just upholding the family motto: I'll do it myself.

When I was fifteen and Les was eight, I almost killed her. We were skiing at Tod Mountain in Kamloops and I took her down an advanced mogul run. I was annoyed to be skiing with my little sister instead of my friends, so I zoomed ahead, not stopping until the bottom. She came barrelling down toward the lift line, knocked over some skiers, disappeared over a ledge, and crashed into a tree.

"Why were you going so fast?" I asked her later, after she'd been evacuated down the mountain, examined, and found to be unbroken. After I'd stopped shaking and berating myself for not looking after her.

"I was trying to catch up," she said.

That evening on the trek, Les and I set up our silver tent in a circular stone compound filled with hay. After dinner, we put on all our clothes against the frozen night, climb into our sleeping bags, and take turns reading aloud from *The Conquest of the Incas*. Reading is something we have in common. We will read by flashlight, by candlelight, by firelight, by moonlight. We will try to read when there is no light at all.

She gives me a hug and bids me goodnight, as if to apologize for her sharpness earlier in the day.

Her black toque peeks out of the top of her sleeping bag. I scoot my mummy-bagged body toward hers for warmth. I can feel the heat coming from her; she's still as hot as the seven-year-old who crawled into my bed after a bad dream.

I wake in the *madrugada* to pee, pull on frozen boots, and walk through mist past a stone enclosure where frosted sheep huddle together. A llama looms out of the dark, stops, sniffs, and moves on. Light diffuses, a peak appears—the sacred snow mountain of Pitusiray.

We begin our final climb up a faint path on the side of a grey scree slope. The rocky trail winds above two lakes the colour of olives. One of the lakes swallowed a boy who came too close with his llamas, Lorenzo says. I walk slowly, drawing in great gulps of thinning air, resting frequently. Les is ahead, chewing coca leaves and moving quickly in spite of her altitude sickness. Maybe the leaves are helping. Lorenzo tells me all the things he has learned that gringos like to know: the kilometres travelled, the distance left to go. At the top of that final pass, we look upon Pitusiray. We are jubilant, having climbed the highest pass on the trek. Lorenzo kneels before the far-off, cone-shaped mountain, offers shiny green coca leaves and a prayer to the mountain spirits, or Apus. Then Leslie moves away from us, sits on a rock, and cries. For Randy, who will only be able to see this place in photos? For the beauty of this wild and sacred pass? For this journey that is ending? For the space between us?

Lorenzo gives her some leaves, tells her to pray to the Apus for help, then leaves her alone. I watch her stare into the mountain's icy face, searching for some sort of solace.

The trail winds down, down, knee-jarringly down. The temperature warms with every thirty metre loss of elevation, and soon we're shedding fleece and toques and Gore-Tex. The waters from Pitusiray follow us downhill in Incan irrigation canals. We come to the lush greenery of the eucalyptus forest, to the clear Cancha Cancha River, then follow the white rapids of the swift-flowing river to Huarán and the highway. Lorenzo flags down a bus. Les and I huddle together in our seat to avoid the swaying of a drunken man who stands in the aisle beside us, losing his balance, falling onto my shoulder and threatening to land in our laps. I sigh, shrug him off. He tips forwards, backwards, and I notice that Les and I are the only ones annoyed. The women with baskets of potatoes, the men in their bright orange-and-red shawls, guide him back to his feet, murmur words of encouragement. Call him *Papá*.

There are stories here to be learned. About a way of caring for each other that we have lost. On the Inca Trail to Machu Picchu, Lorenzo told us a rambling tale about two sisters he was guiding. The younger disappeared, the older frantically searched for her. Found her in a tent with another trekker.

Shivering in a stone hut at 3,000 metres, we waited politely while Lorenzo's story circled around and around, his English, or the way a story is told in Quechua, affecting the retelling. We wanted to leave for the warmth of our down sleeping bags and our book. But we didn't want to be rude.

Back in Cuzco, we invite Lorenzo to a fancy tourist restaurant for dinner. There are candles, white linen tablecloths, an Incan boy playing a mournful song on an Andean wooden flute. Lorenzo seems ill at ease, casts furtive glances at the other diners, eats quickly. We urge him to order dessert. He does, but when the chocolate cake arrives, he carefully wraps it in a napkin to take home to his family.

Outside the restaurant, it is dusk, the sky dark as a new bruise. Lorenzo hugs us, then walks away, turns a corner, and is gone. Without talking, we walk past children peddling postcards of Machu Picchu; women selling treks; tourists fingering alpaca sweaters, holding up fingers and shouting "Best price? Two dollars?" at old women who sit on the cold sidewalk knitting. We return to the Hotel of the Corregidor, climb the dirty, red-carpeted stairs, and get ready for bed. We lie in our separate beds piled with wool blankets, writing in our diaries. Then I take *The Conquest* from the nightstand and in the disappearing light, read my little sister to sleep.

EGGPLANT WITH POMEGRANATE

THE SECOND-LAST TIME I saw M was in the Vancouver restaurant where he worked. We'd stayed up the night before fighting about him going away—to wherever the hell he planned to go: Syria, eastern Turkey, the Kurdish area of Iraq, Iran? He wouldn't tell me. I had to leave that day, to drive back to Alberta where I lived, where I would start a new job, where I hoped he'd move.

He said, "I cannot talk about this any more. Please do not torture me."

August 2002. The North Shore Mountains were stark against the cerulean sky. The trees on his street exploded with green. I went back to his apartment, packed up, slid the spare key under his door, and drove away.

I saw him again, two years later, when I attended a conference in Vancouver. He'd gone wherever he'd gone and returned. The trees were heavy with plum and cherry blossoms. We walked from my hotel on Broadway to False Creek, had fish and chips in a little pub, spoke of his family and mine. I felt our old connection. I felt hope. When I got home, I called. I left messages. He didn't answer.

In 2005, I went to Armenia.

MY CONTACT, ARTHUR, is waiting when my early morning plane lands in Yerevan, the capital of Armenia, a small country bordered by Iran, Turkey, Georgia, and Azerbaijan. We speed through the deserted streets, past classical orange tufa buildings, then up a long hill. Arthur deposits me at a gas station where a tall man is waiting: Evjanik, the husband of Anahit, my host, and a physics professor. I follow him through a dirt field and up crumbling concrete stairs to a Stalin-era building with a dark elevator that jerks us up to the seventh floor.

Anahit greets us at the door. Her crimson hair is as bright as her smile. She is the head of Arevka, a nongovernmental organization dedicated to bettering the lives of Armenian women and children. As a volunteer speech-language pathologist, I will be working with Anahit and Arevka to help children of these families by training local speech-language pathologists in Western techniques.

The table in the dining room is filled with food: eggplant, kebabs, rice, mutton, chicken, pork, salads, and fresh lavash bread. I meet her children: Hasmik, a willowy medical student, and her quiet younger brother, Grigor, a physics major. We sit and Anahit begins to load my plate, a custom I am familiar with, from M. Though I am not particularly hungry, I smile and nod, knowing that it is useless to protest. As a guest, I will be given the tenderest pieces of mutton, the plumpest breasts of chicken, the best of everything.

The following day begins with a leisurely breakfast of fresh lavash, comb honey, roasted eggplant (because I'd said I loved it), boiled eggs, and sharp-tasting sheep's milk cheese.

Anahit washes the dishes, refusing to let me help, the ringing telephone constantly interrupting her. I review my training notes and work plan for the day. At noon, I start to wonder when my workday might start. When I try to ask Anahit, whose English is minimal, she gestures that I should go into the living room and rest.

She serves me a pre-lunch snack of fruit, pastry, and tea. Rose, my interpreter, drops in to meet me. I practise greetings in Armenian.

Later, I hover at the kitchen door, paging through my phrase book, trying to figure out how to ask Anahit about work. She smiles, wipes her hands, leads me back to the living room, turns on the television (perhaps I was asking if I could watch a Russian soap opera?), cuts me an apple just like M used to do, before disappearing back into the kitchen.

Several days later, Anahit and I squat in a crowded *marshrutka* (public minivan) which takes us to Arevka's office in a crumbling concrete high-rise.

"Muslim," says Anahit, pointing to some teenagers playing soccer in the street.

"Really?" I'm surprised, knowing Armenians are mostly Christian.

"Persia."

"They're from Iran?" I ask.

She mimes opening a book.

"Students?"

Anahit nods.

I look at the boys, some in their twenties, and some with the gangly awkwardness of adolescents. They throng around the ball, moving off the road at the last minute for cars, like kids playing road hockey in Canada.

Playing like M did, before the Iranian revolution. As a boy he played street soccer every chance he got. Until, at fourteen, he joined an outlawed leftist student group and his childhood suddenly ended.

I smile at the men chasing the ball down the pothole-filled street, their cries echoing in the warm fall air.

I am waiting to work with Murat, my "demonstration client." The young Armenian therapists are waiting too. The plan is that they'll learn by watching me. Rose will interpret—when she arrives.

Murat is a sweet-natured ten-year-old with large brown eyes, a watchful manner, and a very severe stutter. He moves his head and body, trying to shake out the words. He only speaks when absolutely necessary. His mother, dressed formally in a suit, sits beside him. The student therapists and I smile at each other, Anahit pours us more coffee, Murat's mother straightens his collar. I look through my phrasebook for short words to use in therapy. I've already learned that Armenian has very few words less than three syllables—thank you is the tongue-twisting *shnorhakalutyen*. I pray that Rose will arrive soon.

She doesn't. I show Murat how to breathe using his diaphragm. I use one of my Armenian words to demonstrate how he should start his voice. The therapists giggle at my pronunciation. Murat's mother leans over to me, repeating the word slowly, making me say it until I get it right.

M taught me how to say the more intimate body parts. I have forgotten those words. But I still recognize the sound of his language when I hear it.

We have stopped the car at a roadside stall for more food. Watermelons. Evjanik selects five of the finest, loading them into the already groaning car's trunk. Anahit has been cooking all morning, and the morning and afternoon and evening before, for today's picnic. We continue down a smooth blacktop highway built with Armenian diaspora dollars, the best road I've seen in the country. There's a stop at Areni for bottles of red wine, then at a tomato stall, a melon stall.

Finally, we enter a narrow red rock canyon and arrive at our destination: Noravank, a thirteenth-century monastery perched high on a rocky hill. A priest tours us around the site. He shows us the churches: Surp Astvatsatsin, with its carving of Christ, Peter, and Paul; and the smaller Surp Karapet. Elegant khatchkars (Armenian crosses) carved out of salmon-coloured tufa are arranged artfully around the site. Armenia was the first Christian country in the world. Thaddeus and Bartholomew, two of the seventy apostles, came here to evangelize. Prior to their arrival, Armenia was part of a Persian empire that stretched from Afghanistan to Egypt.

Hasmik, Grigor, and I enter the dark interior of Surp Karapet, its dirt floor dimly illuminated by the flickering of thin candles in sand. They light more candles. I stand back, watching their bowed heads, the soft white of their necks as they pray. We walk out of the church backwards, so as not to turn our backs on God.

Outside, Hasmik poses for my camera. She is dressed like a young North American, in shorts, a spaghetti-strap top, and high-heeled sandals in which she is able to run, negotiate potholes and broken pavement, stand in crowded *marshrutkas*. She cooks, washes dishes, cleans, studies, interprets and translates for me—all this when she is not attending her own lectures or doing shifts at the hospital. She is sweet and even-tempered and I have not once heard her raise her voice to her parents. Grigor is shy and doesn't speak much. He drives the family car, expertly, listening patiently to a barrage of directions from his father I imagine as "careful, watch out for that *marshrutka*, change lanes, turn here, stop at this vegetable stand to get more eggplant for our foreign guest." He has a distant smile and eyes that are often sad. His appearance, his quiet demeanour, his sadness remind me of M.

M told me that before the revolution, before the return of Khomeini, he and his school friends would go hang around a local Armenian church in Tehran to watch the girls.

"They had beautiful eyes," M said. "Like yours."

I have yet to see a blue-eyed Armenian girl.

On the way home from Noravank, we stop at Khor Virap, a monastery above the Araks River. The squat monastery is made of grey stone, surrounded by a wall, one pointed spire topped with an Armenian cross. Evjanik pounds on the locked door and eventually a monk appears and agrees to show us around. In the dying light, I gaze over a sea of green fields, past smoke from outdoor cooking fires to the distant snow-capped peaks of Big and Little Ararat, symbols of Armenia, now across the border in Turkey. "That was our country," says Hasmik bitterly. "Is our country. And we cannot even go there."

M can't return to his country, so he recreated it in his small apartment: the floors were covered with Persian carpets. Stacks of newspapers in Farsi sat in the corners. His bookshelves were filled with Persian books, with the odd Marxist tome in English.

We are visiting the Tsitsernakaberd, the museum of the Armenian genocide. Or rather genocides, for after the first in 1896, they recurred in 1909, 1914, and 1915.

The Ottoman Turks arrested and murdered Armenian men, women, and children, deported them, forced them to march across the desert to Syria. In the museum are photos of skeletal men and women, men hanging from nooses, dead children, piles of skulls and bones. Over a million and a half people were murdered between 1915 and 1923. Many starved to death. The Turks said they were war casualties. Hitler used the Armenian genocide to justify the Holocaust. Because, he said, no one remembered it.

An old man follows us, asks if I am Armenian. I hear Anahit say Canada. What else can I add of my history: That my Scottish great-uncle came to Turkey at the end of World War I to ensure the handover of the country to the Brits, French, and Greeks? That I have seen Atom Egoyan's film *Ararat*, that some of it was filmed in Calgary, where I live? That what I remember most clearly from *Ararat* are the women: women being beaten, women being raped, a mother holding her small boy's hand? That I'd loved a man from a nearby country, a man who had also been tortured, whose colleagues had been killed, who couldn't forget the past?

Anahit says that Armenia is surrounded by enemies. The enemies are Azerbaijan (whose war over Karabagh, a mostly Armenian enclave in the middle of Azerbaijan, could erupt again anytime); Georgia (where they are closing Armenian schools); and Turkey. Iran is Armenia's only friend. Khatami and Ahmadinejad have visited Armenia. There are joint ventures in the works: a gas pipeline from Iran to Armenia, hydroelectric plants, plans for a railway.

Everywhere I go in Yerevan, I see M. Men who look like him. Black hair, brown eyes, moustaches.

Ofelia, Evjanik's sister-in-law, has an Iranian yoga teacher. Anahit has been to Iran several times. Iran is a place I've often imagined but never seen: the Elburz and Zagros mountains, the Caspian Sea, and the Dasht-e Kavir desert.

Armenian music, minor key and mournful, reminds me of the Persian music I used to listen to with M. When the Farsi program would come on the campus radio station, he'd turn up the volume. I knew I wasn't supposed to talk then. I read or I stared out his window at the mountains. He went somewhere else when that program came on; switch backing up a treacherous, rocky path that I couldn't follow.

The food in Armenia reminds me of M. The feta cheese he ate with pita bread for breakfast, the pilau rice dishes like the ones his mother made, the pomegranates he kept in the fruit bowl on his kitchen table, the lemons he ate like they were oranges.

In the crystal fruit bowl on Anahit's coffee table, pomegranates tower over the other fruit. After dinner, Anahit hands me a plate, then takes a pomegranate and prepares it, splitting the red skin, removing the jewel-like seeds, just like M used to do for me. I still find the taste of those seeds too bitter.

There are no overhead transparencies to be had in Yerevan. Or not any that Anahit can locate. I am due to give a lecture about treatment for speech and language disorders at the Pedagogical University and they have promised an overhead projector. Finally, Evjanik finds a store with transparencies and I stay up half the night writing on them.

The next day we enter a cavernous lecture hall featuring a rickety podium and old wooden desks. There is no projector, no microphone. I deliver my lecture as loudly as I can, trying to remember to pause for Hasmik to interpret. I've left fifteen minutes for questions, anticipating a lively intercultural dialogue on the similarities and differences of our treatment techniques. I wait. Silence. There, in the back, is that a hand? No, she's just answering her cell phone. Did they understand me? Was Hasmik's translation audible? I thank them for coming and the audience members file out, talking animatedly among themselves. I am disappointed and puzzled. Why didn't anyone want to talk to me?

At dinner, Anahit is angry that the university couldn't provide a microphone or projector. She cancels the rest of my scheduled lectures there, picks up the phone and begins making arrangements for me to present to therapists at another agency.

Later, I find out she tried for many years to get speech therapy for Grigor. She did find a therapist for him when he was very young. The therapist took little Grigor in the room and shut the door. Anahit was never given any information or invited to participate. I tell her about parent training programs for preschoolers who stutter which are routinely used in Canada and her eyes fill with tears.

I remember the picnic we had at Garni, an old Roman temple outside Yerevan. After our meal, we sat on a blanket under fruit trees, Grigor's head in Anahit's lap, her fingers stroking his thick, black hair.

After M got out of prison in Iran, where he'd been sent for belonging to an outlawed group, he had terrible nightmares. He was afraid to go to sleep. When he screamed in the night, his mother came into his room and held him until he fell asleep again. Though he doesn't live with his parents, they are nearby. I imagine his mom still cooks for him. Who comforts him, though, when he wakes in the night, covered in sweat, shaking?

I spend a day with my translator, Rose, consulting with families and their children and therapists. The children have a variety of speech problems. The families are keen for Western miracles. I wish I had some, but most of the therapy they are getting from the Armenian therapists seems excellent, just what I'd do. I write my recommendations, promise to send requested books and materials when I get home.

I am surrounded by Anahit and Evjanik's friends and relations: her parents, who have arrived from their home in the north, a live sheep trussed in sackcloth in the trunk of their car; Anahit's sister Armineh and her toddler, David; Merineh and her son and daughter; Ofelia.

David is being baptized at Etchmiadzin, the Vatican of the Armenian Apostolic Church. Dressed in our finest on this sweltering autumn day, we wait for the ceremony to begin. Finally, a heavy door squeals open and we are ushered into a dark room with a baptismal font. I stand at the back, but Anahit spots me and leads me to a prime viewing spot in front of the priest. She urges me to take pictures as he pours water over the head of crying David.

After the baptism, we drive to a picnic site at the bottom of a gorge by a tree-shaded stream. The sheep that Anahit's dad slaughtered this morning is being grilled. While the meat is cooking, Ofelia leads me to a place by the stream, and we do yoga poses. When we return, several picnic tables have been put together and are covered with bottles of vodka, wine, brandy, soda, bread, salads, and *khorovats*—skewers of mutton, pork, and chicken.

It is dusk when we sit down to eat. Evjanik, Anahit's father, and the other men make multiple and lengthy toasts to David and Armineh. All these toasts call for frequent topping up of one's glass with vodka. After a few top-ups, I try to keep mine filled with water.

Someone turns on a car stereo. The women pull me up to dance to the mournful music. I try to follow their graceful arm movements, thinking about one New Year's at my sister's place, where M entertained us with a mock belly dance, his arms and hips moving like these women's. David wanders through our midst, clapping his hands, carrying a cucumber, a toy dog, sinking his baby teeth into giant piece of watermelon, laughing as the juice runs down his chin.

I talk to a woman who lived in Iran. She teaches the Iranians who live in the hostel by Anahit's office. She speaks lovingly of her students and Persian culture. I listen carefully, eager to learn what she knows about that country that I have never seen, that I know only from books and movies, from M.

We drive home, in the dark, sated with food and song and dance and the glory of little David, who was passed from hand to hand, from lap to lap, everyone's delight, everyone's beautiful, beloved boy.

I'm visiting the Sarian museum in Yerevan, another excursion arranged by Anahit because I expressed an interest in art. Martiros Sarian was born in Russia in 1880 to Armenian parents. This museum was his home and studio. His paintings are full of yellow light, Yerevan's orange buildings, the salmon-coloured stones of ruined monasteries, the peacock blue of an intense summer sky, the inky black shade. My favourite is called *December in Yarevan*. The foreground features fruits and vegetables—a cornucopia of red pomegranates, grapes, apricots, peaches—orange plains, then blue mountains, plains, mountains, and finally, the snow-capped Mount Ararat.

Sarian witnessed the Armenian genocide of 1915 when he went to Etchmiadzin to help refugees who had fled from Turkey. He travelled in Turkey, Egypt, and Iran, and moved to Russia after the 1917 revolution. There, he devoted himself to painting landscapes of his precious Armenia. He died in Yerevan in 1972 and is buried next to Komitas Vardapet, the famous Armenian monk, composer, and musician. Komitas was rounded up with other Armenian artists and intellectuals in 1915 in Constantinople. He witnessed the death of all his friends. The American ambassador arranged for him to be smuggled to France. Komitas died in a French psychiatric hospital in 1937.

I think about Sarian and Komitas, symbols of this small, spirited country. The one man surviving, prospering, and the other unhinged by the horrors of what he saw.

M had a book full of pictures of men and women. Black-and-white headshots like the photos in my high school yearbook. But his was not a yearbook. It was his book of the dead. The pictures were of students who had been fighting for worker and student rights, who had been murdered by the Khomeini regime. He was lucky, he said, to have been released from prison after only a few months. When he got out, his group helped him escape from Iran.

"I should have died too," he said.

Once we watched the Iranian movie *Children of Heaven*, about a poor boy, Ali, who lost his sister Zahra's shoes.

Because there was no money for a new pair, the children decided to share Ali's sneakers. She would take them in the morning for school, and then run home at noon so he could take them for afternoon class. Ali entered a race hoping to win third prize, which was a new pair of runners. He won first place instead.

"That was beautiful," I said when it ended. "And sad."

"Why?" M asked.

"Because those children, that poor family, had no chance to get ahead, everything was conspiring against them."

"Yes! This is how it is in my country. The workers have no rights, the poor have no rights, students have no rights, children have no rights. The government is . . . is . . . " He stops, overcome with rage.

"I know. My love, I know."

"So you will come with me?"

"I don't even know where you're going."

MY GOODBYE FEAST has been days in preparation. Anahit has scoured the markets for vegetables: tomatoes and onions and squash as big as a head, eggplant and peppers, watermelon and peaches, pomegranates and apples. Anahit and her mother have been cooking for days. Women from Arevka have contributed too: mutton-filled dumplings, meaty cabbage rolls, pastries dripping with honey, and a Persian dish I haven't had before, eggplant stuffed with walnuts and pomegranate.

Finally, Anahit's extended family and I are cheek by jowl around the big dining room table. Evjanik gives a long toast in my honour. Marineh gives me several boxes filled with homemade Armenian pastries which I am to smuggle across the border and eat in front of some Turkish people, a type of revenge I assume. Evjanik offers a bottle of Armenian brandy, also intended to be drunk in Turkey. Ofelia has bought me a silver ring in the shape of a lotus. I begin to cry. I can't stop. What is wrong, they ask, concerned. Are you sick?

I shake my head.

They fill my glass with brandy, pile my plate with more eggplant and pomegranate.

"I love you all" is what I finally manage to say.

"We know," they murmur, crowding around me, patting my back, my hair, as if I am an innocent child. "We love you too."

I hear he has married. I imagine his wife is Persian, someone from his group.

I always thought I'd entered our relationship with my eyes wide open. But maybe they were wide shut, like the Stanley Kubrick movie we saw together.

They were open enough to know he could never be mine. I knew this at the beginning and I loved him anyway.

WHY DON'T YOU REMEMBER ME?

Angkor Wat Temple Complex, Cambodia, 2009

Alighting from our tuktuk, we're thronged by children. "Welcome to Lake Srah Srang," they call. A boy says, "You make me cry" when I won't buy his bangles. Another places two bamboo bracelets into my hand as a "present." "One dollar, Madame, one dollar only," they clamour, holding out their wares. "You rich, you can buy." A girl with a long dark ponytail and bright eyes, who looks to be about eight, suggests I buy a drink at her stall.

"Do you have coffee?" I ask, shivering in the early morning air.

"No. I have Coke, Pepsi, 7up, Mountain Dew, Fanta. Anything you like."

"Too cold. I prefer coffee."

"Okay. You buy later," she says. "When you finish your visit. When hotter."

I shrug.

"You buy."

"Maybe."

"What is your name?"

"Elizabeth."

"You come back, Elizabeth," she insists.

My friends Lynn and Sheila and I walk to the path to the lake, trailed by the chattering children.

"Should we buy something?" asks Lynn.

"No, I read we shouldn't. Their parents take them out of school to sell this stuff."

I take the Lonely Planet guidebook out of my pack, start to flip.

"What does it say?" Sheila asks.

"I'm looking for the page."

"One hundred and fifty-one," says the drink-selling girl. Smarty pants.

"Was there a temple here?" Sheila asks.

"I can't concentrate. These kids are making too much noise."

The drink girl laughs and hushes them in Khmer.

Another tuktuk pulls into the parking lot and the children run over to the new tourists. All but the girl, who sits quietly a few metres away from us as we watch the sun rise over the lake.

"Gorgeous," I say.

"Worth getting up to see," says Lynn. Sheila nods.

"You like?" asks the girl and I nod.

"It is very beautiful," she says and scoots closer.

"Where did you learn English?" I ask.

"From tourists."

"You speak it well."

"Yes. Now you go across road to see Banteay Kdei temple," she bosses, "then you come back and buy cold drink. I am at stall number three. I wait for you, Elizabeth. Do not forget me."

Phnom Penh

On our first day in Cambodia, we visited the royal palace and silver pagoda. The palace was home to the kings of Cambodia. During the Khmer Rouge genocidal regime from 1975 to 1979, King Sihanouk and his family were imprisoned there.

Later, we walked a dirt path along the Mekong River, where teenagers in baggy jeans and soccer jerseys danced to rap from boom boxes. A man led an elephant through traffic, a tiny girl in a pink taffeta dress and shiny black shoes placed jasmine flowers at a Buddhist shrine.

The Khmer Rouge leaders had outlawed colourful clothes and Western dress. The people had to wear black pyjamas with a krama, a checkered Cambodian scarf, wound tightly around their neck.

I read about the trial of Kaing Guek Eav, also known as Comrade Duch, in the *Phnom Penh Post*. The former head of the notorious Tuol Sleng prison, he is the first Khmer Rouge commander to be tried after their leader, Pol Pot, died in 1998 and the Communist regime's remaining soldiers laid down their arms. British journalist Nick Dunlop discovered Duch living freely in northwest Cambodia. He had converted to Christianity and was working for an aid agency.

Our guide to the anthropology museum is Jocelyn. I remember her name because it is also my sister's. Jocelyn shows us statues from the country's Hindu past: the Harihara, a split deity, half Shiva and half Vishnu, shiny from the hands of people wanting good luck.

The Khmer Rouge took children and teenagers like Jocelyn from their parents and forced them to work in the rice fields. Angka, the regime, planned to turn the clock back to year zero, to establish an agrarian workers' paradise, and the young were ripe for brainwashing. The soldiers beat them and forced them to denounce and kill other children. When I was growing up in rural British Columbia, dreaming about boys, going to bush parties, griping about math homework, they were working. Here school was a rice field, and the arithmetic was simple: you worked eighteen hours a day or you died.

Sameth drives us to the Choeung Ek genocidal centre outside of town. His card proclaims him a "good bloke," and informs us that "a safe and fun holiday" awaits us.

He tells us the current Cambodian government headed by Hun Sen does not support the international Cambodian war crimes tribunal. Mr. Sen is a former Khmer Rouge officer. Sameth tells us that former Khmer Rouge soldiers live in his village.

"Are they already out of jail?" Sheila asks.

"No one from the regime has gone to jail. They are completely free. Everyone knows who they are."

"But Duch is on trial," I say. "Surely, he'll go to jail."

Sam shrugs. "Perhaps."

When Sam was one year old, his parents tried to cross a bridge. They started over it several times, but each time he cried so they turned back. They spent the night in the woods. Later, they learned that every person who had crossed the bridge that day was shot.

We pass teenage girls walking hand in hand. Sam says they are going to work in a garment factory. After the factories come fields of emerald morning glory plants, which are harvested for food.

As we walk toward the centre, children's bright voices echo from a nearby schoolyard. The voices trail us on the hard dirt paths around this field. Killing field.

The memorial stupa contains 8,000 skulls.

Seventeen thousand people were murdered here.

A sign tells us that many of the survivors of the genocide have post-traumatic stress disorder. Another sign warns visitors to be respectful of the dead beneath their feet.

I forgot a hat. The sun pummels my head. My feet are sore but I feel like I have to keep going, have to see this. It is my duty to know, to remember.

At the edge of the field, two boys appear. They slide their hands between the fence wires, stare up at us and wait for our coins to fall. How many pieces are needed to absolve us? The Judas West that watched and did nothing.

Siem Reap/Angkor Wat

The streets of Siem Reap, the gateway to Angkor Wat, are thronged with tourists. Pretty Cambodian teenagers hang on the arms of old Caucasian men. We give them the evil eye and a wide berth. The men, I mean. Outside restaurants, Cambodian youth offer cheap food, beer, a good time. Inside the restaurants, older men with missing arms and legs approach us, pressing papers into our hands. The papers describe in English how they lost their limbs to land mines.

In the market, young women sell everything from massages to temple rubbings from nearby Angkor Wat. They stand outside their stalls, calling to us. "Hello, Madame, where you from? You want krama scarf? Silk scarf? Hammock? Come in please, I give you good price."

When I say I'll return later, they call "Okay, Madame. I remember you when you come back. You remember me."

François Bizot is a French, Khmer-speaking scholar. In 1971, he was studying Buddhism in Cambodia near Lake Srah Srang when he was arrested and imprisoned for three months. Comrade Duch was his interrogator. Duch ordered his mock execution. Bizot, armed with early evidence of what the Khmer Rouge could do, tried to warn the French, the former colonial government. They ignored him. In 1975, the Khmer Rouge expelled Bizot and all foreigners from Cambodia and sealed the borders. And for four years, the world ignored this genocide.

Bizot wrote about his experience in his 2003 book *The Gate*—the physical gate, being the one that closed off the French embassy when the Khmer Rouge arrived in Phnom Penh in 1975, and the other, being the gate to the spirit world: "So the gate does not open onto the agonized cries of the tortured in Tuol Sleng prison but onto absurdity and despair . . . This soldier, lying there beneath the stone, is the son or the uncle of someone you know, the lover of the woman you came across, blown to pieces by the side of the road, wearing the new sarong she so carefully chose at the market this morning."

Khem, our guide to Angkor Wat, used to be a monk. He liked the life. The people fed him so his belly was always full. He made friends, travelled. Now, married with two young sons and needing to support his family, Khem makes his living guiding tourists to this World Heritage Site complex of Buddhist/Hindu palaces built between the eighth and thirteenth centuries.

He leads us through the temples, the walls palimpsested with the carvings of each new king, the Shivas and Vishnus and Aspara dancing girls becoming Buddhas becoming Hindu dancing girls again. Khem says that Pol Pot came from a wealthy family. His sister (or was it his cousin?) was a dancing girl, a concubine of the king. This was one reason Pol Pot hated the monarchy. Pol Pot was not so smart, Khem tells us.

He went to France to study radio electronics but failed his exams three years in a row.

Some people want to forget about the Khmer Rouge time, Khem says. Some people do not want to talk about it. Government people especially.

When he retires, Khem tells us, he will become a monk again.

"What about your wife and children?" I ask.

"They will visit me. And they will be with me here," he says, touching his forehead. "I will not forget them."

The Khmer Rouge divided citizens into two groups: the "old people," villagers and farmers, and the "new people," anyone with an education or who supported the old regime. The new people were to be eliminated. The children and teenagers of the new people were to be brainwashed.

I buy a book by Dith Pran called *Children of Cambodia's Killing Fields: Memoirs by Survivors*. In it, Sophiline Cheam Shapiro recalls the propaganda songs she was forced to learn as a child: "I am no different from most of my generation. I know of almost no family that survived without losses. It was a time of the gravest betrayals. Lyrics that promised us the riches of heaven were written by the engineers of our own public hell."

Had we been unfortunate enough to have been Cambodian in 1975, my parents, a doctor and a teacher, would have been murdered. My sisters and I might have survived because we were teens and still considered indoctrinable.

Our tuktuk putts through the peaceful-looking countryside outside Angkor Wat, past houses on stilts, water buffalo, children playing in muddy puddles, chickens and geese, rice fields, buildings sporting logos for political parties,

NGO-sponsored orphanages. The lushly forested and heavily mined Mount Kulen looms in the distance.

Today is a Cambodian holiday and the path to the River of a Thousand Lingas is busy with frisky teenage couples, giggling, smoking, chasing each other. I follow Lynn and Sheila up the trail. It is dusty and steep in places and I know my arthritic knees will hurt on the descent. At the river, we stare with wonder at the sandstone carvings just below the surface: linga and yoni; reclining Vishnu; Shiva and his favourite wife, Uma, on the bull Nandi; Shiva with Uma tucked under his left arm. It is beautiful by the water and we linger, eating fruit, drinking water, and enjoying a shady respite from the blistering heat.

Lynn and Sheila head back down the path. I follow then stop to watch the teens play in the water, splashing each other. I fall on a slippery rock. A young man runs over, offering his hand. Embarrassed, I take it, stand and dust myself off, indicating he and his girlfriend should pass me. They just smile. I start walking, as do they. I stop to take in a view of the river. They wish to enjoy it too, apparently. I stop to drink some water. They are also thirsty. Only when we safely on level ground do they pass me.

In the parking lot, they are waiting for me. I am suspicious, thinking they want money for helping me. But they want to know if I need water, food, a ride; they have a motorcycle and can take me into town. They are acting purely out of kindness and I am ashamed of myself.

OUR GUIDE TO TUOL SLENG in Phnom Penh was tiny. Her suit jacket hung from her body, the sleeve ends obscuring her hands. She was middle-aged. Our age. We trailed her from room to room in this former school turned prison turned genocide museum. In each, there was a new horror to learn. Here the women's long hair was hacked off. There prisoners were photographed and catalogued. In a sunny courtyard, Khmer Rouge soldiers bayoneted babies. In that place where a gentle breeze rippled the grass, men and women and children left for their final journey to the Choeung Ek killing fields outside of town.

People with Vietnamese or Cham blood, foreigners, people over twenty, people with glasses, anyone with an education, an estimated 1.7 million people, were murdered here.

Of the twenty thousand people who were locked up here, only twelve survived.

Our guide was forced to work in the rice paddies. Soldiers broke her legs. She was always hungry. When I was a teenager, planning my glorious future, this woman was making herself too small to be noticed, eating enough bark and leaves so she didn't disappear completely.

I feel nauseated. Sheila's face is very white and Lynn looks distressed. To come here was my idea. I want to apologize but can't seem to find the words.

I try to remember the guide's name. Can't.

I learn that Duch has received a thirty-five-year sentence. It has been commuted to nineteen years for time already served.

Only a few other Khmer Rouge officials will be tried by the international court for genocide.

Duch died in prison in 2020.

THE GIRL AT THE LAKE could be a granddaughter of the children, like Jocelyn, like the prison guide whose name I can't remember, who survived the regime.

Khem confirmed that parents send their children to Angkor Wat to sell trinkets. "If you give them money," he warned, "if you buy from them, they will not go to school. They will have a bad life."

It has been many years since I was in Cambodia and I still remember that girl. Because, you see, after visiting the temple across from Lake Srah Srang, my friends and I returned to our waiting tuktuk. The girl ran out from her stall. She ran to the edge of the highway. She waved furiously as we pulled away. She called out in a high, angry voice: "Elizabeth, you promised me. I wait and wait for you. I remember you. Why don't you remember me?"

WARRIOR ANGELS AND LLAMITAS

AN EARLY MORNING FLIGHT from Buenos Aires brings me to northwest Argentina's City of Perpetual Spring. I've spent five hectic days at a conference and want to escape to somewhere quiet, explore one of Argentina's first Spanish colonial cities and the nearby mountains, mining towns, and indigenous and pre-Hispanic culture.

The Museo de Arqueología de Alta Montaña, the Museum of High Altitude Archeology, displays the mummified bodies of three children discovered by members of an expedition to Mount Llullaillaco, 480 kilometres west of Salta, in 1999. The three are thought to be high-born sacrifices to the Inca gods. For five hundred years they lay two metres beneath the earth, frozen and preserved. The day I visit, the boy mummy is on display: swathed in red, his head to his knees, small hands curled beside his moccasined feet. How old was the boy when he was killed? Did he know of his fate beforehand? Outside, I shiver in the now shady square, drinking a hot chocolate and smiling but shaking my head at a boy selling llamitas, llama dolls made of white wool and decorated with red bows.

The Pajcha Museum of Ethnic American Art features indigenous art and artifacts from the precolonial and colonial periods. The only visitor, I wander through the rooms:

the World of the Andes; World of Beliefs; the Mapuche World; the World of the Inhabitants of the Mountains and Plains. Examine masks, clay figures, dolls, indigenous jewelry and textiles. Diego, the elegantly dressed vice-director, appears and offers me a free English tour. He talks at length about the *ángeles arcabuceros*, warrior angels painted by European-trained indigenous artists of the Cuzco (Peru) school. Demon-fighting warrior angels are usually depicted as soldiers. These brightly coloured paintings feature men in aristocratic seventeenth-century Spanish dress: elegant coats, breeches, and wide, feathered hats. No ordinary gentleman, however, they sport angel wings and carry muskets instead of the traditional sword, as painted by the artists of the Cuzco school who liked them for their resemblance to their ancient gods and heroes.

Intrigued by the warrior angels and their Incan painters, I sign up for a day trip to the UNESCO World Heritage Site Quebrada de Humahuaca because it includes a visit to a church with paintings of *ángeles arcabuceros*. We are on the road by 7 a.m., our van speeding up Highway 9 to the outdoor handicrafts market in Purmamarca, where women sell scarves and hats, llamitas and ponchos, their serious-looking children silent beside them while tourists paw through their wares, asking for this colour or that.

We continue up through the Quebrada de Humahuaca. The narrow valley is on the Camino Inca from Lima to Buenos Aires, and once connected Salta with the rich silver and gold mines at Potosí and Oruro, Bolivia, which I've visited: the Spanish benefitting from the poorly paid labour and deaths of thousands of indigenous miners. The Quebrada was the first part of Argentina to be colonized by the Spanish. The valley has been a trade route from the high mountains to the temperate plains for tens of thousands of years. I'm struck by the striations of the sedimentary mountains that line our route. They remind me of Drumheller—that is if nature had painted the badlands with alternating zigzag swaths of sage and emerald green, lilac, cream, magenta, and carmine.

At 2,989 metres, the town of Humahuaca, a stopping point en route to the high altiplano, is warm in the sun but chilly in the shade. Our guide, Gaston, announces that we have "free time for shopping." I prefer to visit the seventeenth-century Iglesia de Nuestra Senora de la Candelaria y San Antonia, hoping for warrior angels. There are twelve prophets painted by Marcos Sapaca of the Cuzco school but no *angelitos*. Nearby are cactus-lined stone steps leading to the heroes of the independence movement monument. The centrepiece of the large sculpture is a local indigenous leader, Diego Viltipoco, his bronze arm raised in victory in the nineteenth-century war for independence from Spain. Seventy tons of bronze went in to the making of the sculpture.

Nine paintings of *ángeles arcabuceros* line the walls of the pretty white San Francisco de Paula church in the nearby village of Uquía. I sit in a simple wooden pew, scanning the paintings and gilded seventeenth-century altar. Did the conquistadors consider the indigenous people demons? The very people who should have called *them* devils?

On the way back to Salta, we stop at the Pucará de Tilcara, the fortress ruins of the Tilcara people, who lived as shepherds and farmers from 1000 until the conquistadors arrived and arrested Chief Viltipoco in 1594. The Tilcara bred llamas, which served as pack animals and provided meat, and hunted their cousins, vicuñas and guanacos. Sacred animals were sometimes sacrificed to the gods to ensure a good harvest. The Tilcara were forced into indentured labour by the infamous Spanish *encomienda* system.

Another day, another tour: I find myself in the village of Santa Rosa de Tastil in the Quebrada del Toro, again with "free time to shop." I wander through a handicraft market in the plaza where the local women stand quietly watching. The guide points out a house where the local shaman meets with residents. No warrior angel on guard here. The only sign, the one above the splintered wooden door, instructs people to "wait in silence." No one waits, though I can hear muffled voices from inside.

In the mining town of San Antonio de los Cobres, the dirt streets and adobe houses are surrounded by mountains containing copper, iron, and lead. I walk the streets, tailed by silent children holding llamitas. Which I don't buy. I don't really need or want to carry more souvenirs, don't have any children or grandchildren to give one to. Though I should. Buy one. To help the children and their families.

Back in the van, the road becomes dirt. Gabi, our guide, stops so we can photograph the white llamas that wander the plains, walking toward them to try to get a good picture until they startle away. One hundred dusty kilometres later, we arrive at the *salinas grandes*, lakes covered in salt up to half a metre thick. Donning sunglasses to protect my eyes from the blinding white of the lakes, I watch the salt miners working in rectangular basins. They make thirty-five pesos, less than five dollars, for a ton of salt, two days of backbreaking work. Mining companies, including ones from Canada, want to mine lithium here. The indigenous communities are opposed. Lithium mining will rob their communities of the water they depend on for their llamas and sheep.

Back in town outside the archeology museum, a serious,

big-eyed boy holds out a llamita. I smile, look at his red poncho, his plastic-sandalled feet, and shake my head. The sun is going down and the evening air is chilly. I notice that his mother, guardian angel, watches silent from her blanket of handicrafts on the stone ground. Buy it, I tell myself. I take out a few pesos, and drop them into his waiting hand.

MEMORIA, JUSTICIA, SIN OLVIDO

When will I be home? I don't know.In the mountains, in the rainy night,The autumn lake is flooded. Someday we will be together again.We will sit in the candlelight by the west window,And I will tell you how I remembered youTonight, on the stormy mountain.

—Li Shang Yin

The Border

The bus passes through yellowing vineyards along Route 7, traces of the old route palimpsested onto the landscape. To my right are dry, sage-coloured hills, like the ones outside Kamloops where I grew up. Then we're beside a river which could be the Kicking Horse meandering down the valley to Field. Karin and I stopped in Field one scorching afternoon on our way home from a kayaking trip, soaking our feet in the icy water.

But I am not in Canada with my friend. I am on an Argentinian bus heading for the Chilean border.

The road climbs steeply, the sides of the mountains littered with abandoned snow-moving equipment. Passing the entrance to Mount Aconcagua and the deserted Los Penitentes ski area, named for the ice forms resembling people praying, it begins to snow.

Inside the restaurant of the climbers' refuge which is our lunch stop, I find a place at the long table surrounded by open-flamed gas heaters, which waiters occasionally nudge as they rush in and out of the kitchen bearing steaming pots. It is cozy and communal, the kind of place Karin would have loved.

Susana, from Córdoba, asks what I am doing in Argentina. I tell her I was in Buenos Aires for a conference and am taking some time to explore her country before visiting a friend in Bolivia. Yes, I say, alone.

Wandering through the market at Inca Bridge, I stroke the colourful woollen mittens and hats. If Karin were here, I would buy them for her.

Back in Mendoza, yellow leaves line the streets, crunching underfoot. I wander into a "people's festival." Vendors sell empanadas and ice cream. Children chase each other around a fountain. A woman sings "Gracias a la Vida" in a haunting alto voice.

Karin sang beautifully—in Spanish, English, her native German, Mandarin. Everything from "Guantanamera" to "The Happy Wanderer." She was in two choirs. We sang together at her home in Canmore, on hiking trails. When I sang with Karin, I felt at peace. I snuck away from my conference to go to the Plaza de Mayo. I was hoping to see the mothers and grandmothers marching in their white scarves and baby shawls printed with the names of their missing children and grandchildren. Missing since Argentina's Dirty War (1976–1983) when thirty thousand activists were tortured and murdered by General Videla's thugs. But the plaza contained no marching women, only the odd tourist wandering the vast plaza in front of a scaffolded government house.

At the corner of the plaza, there is a white banner. I imagine it was left by the mothers and grandmothers. It reads: *Memoria Justicia sin Olvido*. Memory, justice, never forget.

TWO YEARS AGO, I sat in the front row of the Policeman Creek hall in Canmore waiting for Karin's memorial service to begin. I didn't want to talk to anyone because I didn't want to cry, so I sat and stared at my eulogy. Somehow I caught a glimpse of Karin's mother, Felicitas, recently arrived from Germany. She saw me. She called my name. My fragile composure crumbled. In what world should a mother outlive her daughter?

Salta

There are supposed to be two children and one teenager here but only one body is on display today. He wears a scarlet tunic, a white feather crest on his bent head. This boy is one of the three mummies found two metres beneath the snow on the summit of the Llullaillaco volcano near the border with Chile. Thought to be sacrifices, they are now displayed at this museum. As I stare at the boy, I wonder what it took for his parents to offer him up. Did they have a choice? Or was he just taken from them?

Outside the museum, I see a parade of *descamisados*: Evita Perón's "shirtless ones," young people banging drums in support of the Perónista candidate in the coming election. While travelling through Argentina, I am reading about Evita.

How she grew up in poverty, left her town to work as a radio actress, met and married political strongman Juan Perón. How she worked to help the poor and dispossessed. At age thirty-one, Evita was diagnosed with cervical cancer. She died two years later. People still pay homage to "Santa Evita." The ground outside her crypt in Buenos Aires's La Recoleta Cemetery is blanketed with flowers.

KARIN'S ASHES are scattered in the Alberta mountains she loved: at Peaceful Point near Dead Man's Flats, at Memorial and McArthur Lakes. I have a picture of the tree her husband, Jacob, and sister, Ulli, decorated in her honour, with cards and a photo of her in an orange poncho in front of a waterfall, the tree festooned with wildflowers.

San Lorenzo

Once in a while, I forget I am no longer young. I forget what my middle-aged body can no longer do easily. This morning, I thought it could still pull me up and down muddy mountain slopes of the Reserva del Huaico cloud forest. But I am easily winded, and my knees are burning. My guide finds me a stick, offers his hand on the slippery sections. He pauses, ostensibly to point out the view but really to let me catch my breath. At the end of the hike, he waits with me for half an hour until my taxi back to town arrives. This young man helps me into the back seat as if I am his own mother.

KARIN AND I MET in our twenties. We shared books, discussed our writing. We hiked and backpacked, skied and kayaked. She was supremely fit, climbing many peaks in the Rockies, traversing the Alberta ice fields on skis. We shared a love of travel and languages. While I learned Spanish and travelled in Mexico, Cuba, and South America, she learned Mandarin and travelled solo in China, kayaked in Greenland, Florida, the Yukon. With an all-male Polish crew, she sailed across the Atlantic. She backpacked in Alaska and lived in a remote cabin in Fairbanks while interning for the local paper.

We were roommates. She cooked for me. She taught me how to cook. She taught me how to meditate. Karin was one of the most energetic and positive people I knew, and when I spent the weekend with her in Canmore, I always came home happy and full of hope.

Growing up, I was shy, preferring books to people. As a child, I don't remember having a best friend, an intimate I could tell anything to. As an adult, I did.

When she was thirty-four, Karin was diagnosed with advanced breast cancer. She had the most aggressive treatment available at the time: mastectomy, regular chemo, high-intensity chemo, a bone marrow transplant, radiation. I thought she was cured. Karin thought she was cured. Twelve years later her cancer returned. The doctors gave her six months to live.

Karin did everything she could to survive, eating organic and low-glycemic foods, using natural products, doing naturopathic as well as conventional treatments, praying, meditating, writing. From the minute of her recurrence, she lived intentionally. She travelled to a Santa Barbara medical centre founded by Dr. Carl Simonton, an oncologist who pioneered a method of emotional support for cancer survivors. She and Jacob travelled to Germany to visit her family, to Greece. If she ever gave in to grief, which she must have, I never saw it. When I'd call, she'd want to talk about me, what I was doing, reading, writing, where I was hiking or skiing, about our mutual friends. When she was tired, she asked if I would please let her go.

Two months before she died, we went out for lunch. On a sunny December day, we ate eggplant sandwiches at Crazy Weed restaurant in Canmore and reminisced about our kayaking trip. The storm that caught us on Sugar Lake, forcing our kayak onto boulders where we huddled in wet clothes waiting for the wind and waves to die down so we could paddle back to our campsite beneath the dark cliffs of Thompson Lake.

After lunch, we went for a short hike. I noticed how winded Karin was, how thin her legs were. Back at her house, she made us a snack. "I'm eating all the time," she told me, laughing. "Avocados, almond butter: all the good fat." She had a coach, Alan, who had survived cancer, helping her. "He says I can't afford to lose any more weight."

Until then, I hadn't seriously entertained the idea that my friend might die. I knew her situation was grave. Until that day in December, I thought she might be one of those miraculous cases you read about. Because she was working so hard to live, had already survived a year longer than the doctors predicted, I thought my friend, who climbed so many mountains, could summit one more.

I have a binder with recipes Karin gave me over the years. Some she cooked for me when we lived together. Some she gave me when I visited her in Canmore and raved about something she'd made. Healthy, easy (because she knew I was a lazy and indifferent cook), and tasty recipes, with her comments written neatly below: tagine marrakech ("superb!"), pollo guisado ("add molasses to get darker colour"), ginger beef stir-fry with pasta ("nice garlic/ginger combination"), pesto sauce ("tasty and healthy"), carrots with basil ("an excellent way to cook carrots").

Karin organized and added to my meagre spice collection. She bought me things she insisted every kitchen needed: a wooden spoon, a wok, a set of Chinese rice bowls.

After her second diagnosis, my friend started a blog called Healthy Survivor. Two months before Karin died, she wrote: "By no means do I expect the medical treatment to be the 'long term cure,' and, statistically, there is no guarantee (of) that. . . . The absolute final healing is up to the highest power I know of, and that is God. In a way this is a valuable lesson in humility. We are only human. We do not have all the answers. We are not all powerful. We are not in control of everything. However, this should not make us fearful or despairing. It opens us up to the possibility of GRACE."

Her last post, in December 2009, began: "This month, I feel like I have been wandering between grievance and gratitude. However, gratitude prevails."

WIND DASHES THE LAST of the leaves from the trees and hurls them through the streets. My friend Richard picks me up at the airport and drives me to his apartment. Like Karin, he's a great cook and the fresh fruit smoothie he has prepared for me is followed by oven-roasted chicken, mashed potatoes, and flan.

I go with him to his university, hang out in the teachers' lounge while he lectures, practising my Spanish with the friendly profs. Later, we walk the market streets of Santa Cruz looking for a part to fix his shower so I can have hot water. I tell him I don't need hot water. He insists that I do.

One night, Richard tells me that I was one of the last people to see his dying mother, Caridad, when I visited her while on a study trip to Cuba. He tells me that every day he thinks about her, every day he misses her, all his work is for her.

I tell him about Karin. And once I start to talk about my friend, I can't stop. I feel like I've just received the bad news from Jacob. I talk for hours. I use up all of Richard's tissues. Later, I soak his sheets with my tears. I feel as lonely and desolate as I've ever been in my life.

The next day I apologize.

"Why?" he asks.

"For being so sad."

"Don't be sorry," he says. "It is normal."

Buenos Aires Again

An erupting volcano near the Chilean border has closed the airport. The air is hazy with ash. I spend my days wandering the city, my evenings reading Tomás Eloy Martínez's *Santa Evita*. Despite Evita's suffering at the end of her life, she still wanted to help her countrymen and women solve their problems, bring them justice. I think about the mothers and grandmothers in the plaza—how not knowing what happened to their sons and daughters, granddaughters and grandsons must haunt them. I think about the people Karin left behind: her husband, her twin sister, her brothers. Her mother, Felicitas. Her father, Franz. Aunts and uncles and cousins and in-laws and so many friends.

Karin's motto in the last months of her life was no more unnecessary suffering. Is there necessary suffering? Is what I am feeling necessary? And I wonder why it is here, in Argentina, that I remember Karin so strongly. Is it because of reading about Evita and her cancer, the *madres* and their lost children? Or because this is the way grief works: sneaking up on you when you least expect it, while you are perusing knitted goods in a market, listening to a sad song, looking out the window at a mountain river—knocking you flat, leaving you desperate and alone.

I resolve to work against despair. If my friend could find gratitude while dying, I will look for comfort in the places Karin found it. In meditation and music, in nature and spirituality. In books, friends, and family. I will leave my head and look out the window at the glorious yellow-leaved poplar trees. I will remember that I still have a body, arthritic knees and all. I can still walk. And while walking, I recall the morning Karin and I climbed from our campsite to the top of North Molar Pass, down from the top of the world to golden larches emerging from the mist below.

I LEARN THAT THE BANNER in the plaza, *Memoria Justicia sin Olvido*, is the slogan of continental veterans of the Malvinas or Falklands war, many of whom suffer from post-traumatic stress disorder. They are asking for pensions, for the government to compensate them for their suffering. The veterans are supported by many Argentine organizations including the Madres. They are asking for justice.

AND SO I REMEMBER: Karin and me sitting side by side, drinking green tea, and reading to each other from our respective books. Hauling stones together to make a "rock river" through her yard. Climbing Jewell Pass in the pouring rain, jumping out of the way for mountain bikers.

I read the little book she made for me with her favourite poems and sayings called "Bright Days Ahead." This verse by T'ao Ch'ien:

Swiftly the years, beyond recall.
Solemn the stillness of this fair morning.
I will clothe myself in spring clothing
And visit the slopes of the eastern hill.

By the mountain stream a mist hovers,
Hovers a moment, then scatters.
There comes a wind blowing from the south
That brushes the fields of new corn.

Karin's words are written beneath: "Despite the feeling of sadness because of the passage of time, there is always hope for something new."

On the day after Karin's memorial service, I went up to the Canmore Nordic Centre. I skied up Banff Trail and then climbed a trail that led into the trees. At the top of the smaller trail, I stopped for a rest. Flying downhill, I felt my friend beside me. She was there, just for a moment. And then she was gone.

Driving back to Calgary, I turned on radio to Pete Seeger singing "Guantanamera." Perhaps that, too, was a gift.

THE ART HOSPITAL, THE FLOATING HOSPITAL, AND THE BURNING HOUSE

THE ART HOSPITAL SMELLED of sandalwood. A boy in a white knee-length shalwar kameez and a fez patrolled the common room with a censer. An old, bearded man swept the white floors and lit the tall silver candles at their corners. At night, stars shone from the ceiling like the cutouts in a Turkish hammam I once visited. I should have liked the art hospital but I didn't. It was lonely as hell.

We patients had to attend daily lectures. We sat captive in a row of plastic seats, their high sides obscuring us from one another. One day a woman who strangely looked like my artist cousin, Charlotte, told us how painting had healed her. She showed us slides of her work but the slides were small and my glasses had disappeared. After the lecture, I tried to get out of my chair but my belly was suddenly too swollen. I couldn't speak, either, so I rang and rang my call bell. I stared at the artist, hoping she'd notice I needed help. She didn't. Finally, the boy came and tried to lift me. He made a rude comment about me being too out of breath. What did he mean? This was supposed to be a rehabilitation hospital. Where were my rehabilitators?

I'd had just about enough of the art hospital. I wanted to go back down to the regular hospital. But the director insisted I stay. She was tall and willowy, a Balinese dancer in a gold-and-emerald sarong, her black hair swept into an inverted cone. The dancer danced, extended her Olive Oyl arms, waved her hips back and forth—a shadow puppet at the edge of the room. I kicked and kicked my bed. Let me out of here.

Finally, an orderly appeared. He pressed a button and my bed slid down a chute to the regular hospital. All I had to do was transfer myself to a gurney on the other side. The bed was close, just a few centimetres away, but I couldn't move. There was no one to help me. Exhausted, I gave up. My bed whirred back up to the art hospital.

This time I was in a large cave staffed by Mexican physiotherapists. The walls were decorated with bark paintings of deer and corn dancers. Beaded Huichol gourd bowls sat on the tables. There were roosters, too, but they didn't move, so they must have been sculptures of roosters. The women seemed cheerfully resigned to an overly busy workday, to unpaid overtime, though I heard one talking about filing a grievance with the union.

My physiotherapists manoeuvred my swollen body into various positions, resting me on their strong backs when I was tired. I liked this part of the art hospital better. But I was damned if I was going to stay here.

TOXIC DELIRIUM IS a sudden, confused state of mind that comes and goes and affects personality and behaviour. People with this condition have trouble paying attention to what is going on around them and doing the things they normally do. It can be caused by a number of things. In my case, an emergency operation.

In the ICU, I had a private nurse who had come all the way from Seattle to look after me. This nurse called me Little Bear, which was funny because that was what my sister Leslie sometimes called me. The nurse kept trying to get me to breathe deeply, which was annoying because I already knew how to breathe. I thought it strange that the nurse was staying with my friends Angelika and Garrick. That she came to the hospital in Garrick's borrowed truck, which used to belong to a national park warden and had a cage in the back for transporting bears. In fact, it was uncanny how much the nurse looked like my sister Leslie, who was also from Seattle.

ONE DAY MY FAVOURITE NURSE, Leanne, told Leslie and me a story. While on vacation in Mexico, she'd seen a fire burning on top of a mountain. A series of burning huts, she was told. A ritual. Before a Huichol woman gave birth, she was put in the last hut. The first hut was set on fire. The woman had to have her baby before the fire reached her hut. Then, the newborn strapped to her belly, she cooked a feast for her family.

Seven months later, I can find no reference to this Huichol birth ritual. In a 2013 article in the academic journal *Social Science & Medicine*, however, entitled "Shame as a Barrier to Health Seeking among Indigenous Huichol Migrant Labourers," I learn that indigenous Huichol women usually give birth alone or with a *mara'akame,* a shaman, present. According to medical anthropologist Dr. Jennie Gamlin, many Huichol people believe that "while western medicine may cure the illness, it will not treat the cause, this will always be supernatural and any illness treated bio-medically will also require a spiritual cure." One of Gamlin's interviewees, Graciela, explained: "When the baby can't come out because the Nenekate and Kaka+yarixi (gods) won't let it through, this is when the mara'akame opens the doors, by speaking to them."

My parents and I once took a tour to a Huichol community outside Puerto Vallarta. Our guide, Miguel, and a shaman, Santi, took us through Santi's village, where we visited the church with its altar of deer antlers, bow and arrows, and gourd bowls called *xukuri*. *Xukuri* are symbolic wombs that are filled with blood offerings to the gods. They are used to contact the spirit world.

The Huichol believe their beings are formed by elements of the natural world: fire, air, water, earth. Plants, deer, and maize are ancestor gods who can be accessed through ingesting peyote. Peyote visions inspire their art: yarn paintings and beaded *xukuris*. A shaman artist may sacrifice a deer, and inhale its last breath, before creating a piece of art.

In Santi's village, my father bought a *xukuri*. I purchased a yarn painting: a green shaman with horns holding a medicine bundle and a torch, a deer below, birds at the four corners. The painting hangs at the entrance to my living room.

MY DOCTORS WORRY about my cognitive status, my fluctuating level of orientation. I am wheeled down long corridors, lifted on and off gurneys by singing Mexican porters. My body is slid into CT and MRI caves. Hot liquid whooshes through my abdomen. A disembodied voice tells me to hold my breath. How? I gasp for air. My butterfly lungs are missing their bottom wings.

In the ICU, nurses ask what I need. I'm getting good at gestures. Moving my shoulders upward means reposition me on the bed. Pointing to my mouth means suction. Pointing combined with a hands-up shrug means when will this damned breathing tube be removed? "Not yet, not yet," they say. "Your lungs are full of fluid. You can't breathe by yourself."

Leslie builds me an altar with pictures from my travels: a white Buddha, Indian and Indonesian textiles, a red Colima dog. She writes a bit about me on the whiteboard. She finds me an alphabet board so I can communicate more than yes and no. When I spell "sisters" for the nurses, it means Where are they? When are they coming? My sisters, Leslie, Jocelyn, and Melissa, are allowed to arrive early, stay late, because I am less anxious and agitated when they are with me. When I wake, open frightened eyes, Les talks gently, calling me back from wherever I've been.

Doctors come and go, wanting to know where I am. A difficult question. Where I am floats toward then away from me, a piece of driftwood. Sometimes I am in a hospital on the top of a mountain in Colorado. Sometimes I am in Calgary, but at the South Health Campus with the floor-to-ceiling windows that look out onto brown prairie. Sometimes I am where I am, the Peter Lougheed Hospital.

The ICU doc weans me off the psychotropic drugs he thinks are causing my alterations of consciousness. He brings a machine to suck the fluid out of my lungs, urging me to watch the screen. My lungs are full of green liquid, floating ferns snared on bones. We got twenty litres, Dr. Luc announces proudly. Twenty litres, I think. Enough to drown in.

I WOKE UP ON FEBRUARY 21 feeling exhausted. Thought I'd overdone it with two days of cross-country skiing at Lake Louise the previous weekend. I'd been tired all week. On Friday I overslept, dressed quickly, walked to work. I had just turned on my computer when I felt a sharp pain in my lower back. My skin turned clammy. Something in my belly let go, like a stitch unravelling. I called a friend to bring me home.

I lay in my bed thinking that the hard bed in the Lake Louise hostel, combined with lack of stretching before and after skiing, had caused the back pain. Then the back spasms turned into stabbing knives. I threw up red-brown liquid. Staggered to the phone and made an appointment with my doctor, called my friend to take me there.

At the clinic, the resident couldn't find my blood pressure. Tried a second machine. A third. The knives were tearing me to pieces now. I remember screaming. Being given an IV for pain. An ambulance ride. Pain dissolving. A CT scan. A doctor told me I had to have emergency surgery. Another woman asked if I wanted to see a social worker, the chaplain. No chaplain. Yes, social worker. I told her to call my one of my sisters. I knew they'd call each other and my elderly parents who didn't hear well on the phone.

In a different ambulance. A man asking me my name, where I live, when I was born. Already told you. But he kept asking, flooding my eyes with light, when all I wanted to do was sleep.

This man, I learned later, was the Foothills ER doctor. He had jumped into the ambulance because he wasn't sure I'd survive the ride to the Lougheed, where they were prepping for my surgery. Because at ten o'clock that morning, a

9.5-centimetre aneurysm—a ballooning of the aortic artery in my abdomen—burst, flooding my belly with blood. I'd had a triple A: an abdominal aortic aneurysm. Known as the widow-maker because it usually happens to elderly men, who usually die. Half of the blood in my body poured into my peritoneum. The social worker told my family I had a 10 percent chance of surviving the emergency surgery, where a stent would be inserted through my femoral arteries. My chances of surviving after the operation were 4 percent.

I was given blood, litres and litres of it. Six transfusions in all.

THE SNOW HAD STARTED Saturday night and was still falling heavily in Lake Louise by Sunday morning. Pipestone Trail had been track set the day before, but the tracks were obliterated. I clamped my boots into my cross-country skis and followed my friends up the trail, my skis gliding easily on fresh snow. The trees wore crowns of snow, shoes of earth. The four of us moved over frozen ground, through the beautiful silent world.

THE PETER LOUGHEED HOSPITAL could float. Was, in fact, a hospital ship that nightly sailed down the Elbow River. I was inside the boat, though I yearned to be outside on the deck. Wanted to watch our dark passage, hear the lapping of the water, see the stars. But my fellow passengers, nurses all, wouldn't let me get up. Kept telling me to calm down. Sleep, sleep. Go back to sleep.

Leslie told me later that I had been taken from surgery to a windowless ICU room, a little cave. When they moved me to a room with big windows and stars on the ceiling, my orientation improved and I stopped trying to remove my tubes.

One night I was drowning in fluid. I rang and rang my call bell but no one came. I kicked and kicked my bed and still nobody came. Then finally someone did. She checked my lines, my oxygen levels. I pointed to my mouth, my throat. *I can't breathe. Suction me!*

Les told me later there had been three code blues in ICU that night. Three people's hearts stopped. Three people floated out of the world.

Scotty, my favourite respiratory therapist, was on duty the spring day I passed the spontaneous breathing test, the day my breathing tube was finally removed. I coughed ferociously, like a wounded beast, gasping and wheezing between bouts. After the coughing abated, I tried out my voice. It was bearish, a low-pitched whisper-growl.

Scotty's wife and daughter arrived to perform dances of universal peace for patients. They wore long embroidered robes and colourful scarves. While Leanne looked for a place for them to dance, the girl wordlessly approached me, handed me a red rose.

I fell asleep and when I woke up the dancers were gone. I'd missed them. I asked Leanne when they would return. "Pardon me?" she asked. Apparently, there were no dancers in the hospital.

Later that day, I insisted that my sister Melissa call our parents because my mother was lost. For some reason, Mel wouldn't do it. A doctor came with a CPAP breathing machine, covered my face with a mask. I kept trying to pull it off. Mel begged me to wear it, said I wasn't getting enough oxygen and if I didn't wear it, they might have to put the breathing tube back in. I stopped fighting and went sailing instead, this time on a sleek sailing ship, tacking into the wind, heading out to sea.

I was transferred from ICU to a ward, and then discharged. My sister Jocelyn installed equipment in my home: bath bars, raised toilet seat, a pole I could use to pull myself up from the couch. She gave me a bell, which I rang ten, twenty times a night. I started coughing again, couldn't stop, couldn't get enough air. Joc called my doctor, who told her to take me to Emerg. I had pulmonary emboli, tiny clots starring my lungs.

Five days later and stabilized on blood thinners, I came home for the final time. My eighty-six-year-old mother came to look after me. She insisted that I do my breathing exercises hourly, made me walk. Supervised me, as I slowly inched my walker down the sidewalk, pushing it through thawing earth and tiny shoots of green to a bench in my neighbourhood park. My belly was still huge, full of the blood that had flooded it when my aorta ruptured. My surgeon, Dr. Nutley, told me that the blood would eventually reabsorb—that slowly, slowly my belly would shrink to its normal size.

In June I told a writer friend about the art hospital. She wondered if I had gone there when I was leaving my body. It had been touch-and-go for me the first few days in ICU. Was that the night I tried to go back from the art to the regular hospital but couldn't, the night of the three code blues? The night Leslie was tugged awake at 3:00 a.m., got into the bear truck, and raced to the hospital?

IN JULY, I SWAM in Okanagan Lake. Drove my parents' car down the rutted entrance road to Kalamoir Park, past ponderosa pines and quails. Donned my bathing suit and water shoes and dove in. My nervous parents paced the shoreline, making sure my head stayed above the surface. I loved being back in water, though the lake was disturbed, rocked by currents and stirred by the winds. Ferns brushed against my legs; ducks swam by, dropping feathers.

I returned to Kelowna in August. Kalamoir Park was closed because of fires. Smith Creek, across the road from my parents' home, was burning. My parents were on evacuation alert, had the car packed with valuables, and were ready to leave at a moment's notice. At night, they set up lawn chairs on the street, watched the flames jump from tree to tree. There was fire all around them, ash dropping onto lawns and swimming pools, but somehow all of the houses were spared.

Leslie told me Leanne had been in Mexico but hadn't told us the story about the fire on the mountain. But I still wonder if the woman in the burning hut I imagined had her child before her blood womb broke and the fire reached her home. Did a shaman help to let the baby out? Once her waterbaby was born, did the woman strap the tiny girl to her chest and cook that feast for her relatives, as I would, later, for my family and friends who'd kept vigil, who called me back?

In Huichol mythology, the earth is a pregnant female belly that contains and produces life. Earth was created from the gourd womb of the earth goddess, Tatéi Yurianaka, when Kauyumari, the trickster, entered her womb and enlarged her belly. The ancestral gods and goddesses then created a flood of blood that filled the earth womb and carried them gently back to the surface of the world.

Back on this shifting surface, I know the line between myth and truth is blurred, that consciousness can have many levels. I lived in many different places during my illness, and I came back to this shining world knowing that nothing is absolute, everything is constantly shifting, all I can do is be thankful and enjoy the journey to come.

THE DESERT BY THE OCEAN

April, 2022

"*Quién es la señorita*?" the cab driver asks, sneaking mirror peeks at Ayuko while he is supposed to be driving.

"What is he saying?" asks Ayuko.

"He wants to know who you are."

"Tell him I'm your adopted niece."

I don't have an adopted niece, but this tiny beauty, twenty-four years my junior with a butterfly tattoo on her wrist and a penchant for purple, plants, and locally sourced, gluten-free organic food, could be her.

Ayuko and I were supposed to go to Thailand together. But post-pandemic flights to Thailand were expensive, and Covid cases there were climbing as fast as Thai temperatures in April. Plus, it was Songkran, the Thai New Year, and it would be crowded.

I told her I'd been to the Mexican Baja many times and the Covid numbers where we were going were low. The flight to Loreto is short, I speak Spanish. We could visit my Calgary friends, Rosita and Doug, who have a condo outside of town. Truth be told, it was my first choice.

"But I've been so looking forward to Thailand," she said.

"We can go when the pandemic is over. I'm sixty-two. I have some health issues. If I get Covid, it could be bad for me."

"But I really, really want to go to Asia."

"And I really, really don't want to get sick," I countered.

As a hairdresser turned health-care aide, she knows about Covid. Mexico it was.

The Mexicans are intrigued and confused by her. They ask me about her ethnicity and Canadian doesn't satisfy. No, not Korean, not Filipina. Japanese, yes, also Chinese. "*Una mezcla*," I say, a mixture, and this seems to satisfy.

"How did you meet her?" they ask, perhaps because she is young and Asian and I'm not.

"She's my hairdresser."

They don't ask why I am travelling with my hairdresser (my short, easy cut does not require daily styling or weekly colouring, though Ayuko wishes I attended to it more regularly). We met fourteen years ago when I walked into the salon where she rented a chair. I liked how she cut my hair. She slowly convinced me to shorten and modernize the bob I'd had for years. I followed her when she moved salons. I learned to trust her creative instincts and let her do what she likes with my hair, as a good aunt might.

I am not sure why I am travelling with my hairdresser except she asked me to. Because I had more travelling experience and we had hiked and camped together, perhaps. I worried about the age difference, that she might be bored with me and my penchant for reading a lot and going to bed early, that she might be too reliant on me, having never travelled independently before. On the plus side, I told myself, she is small but mighty, fun and lively. Bonus: she can lift heavy objects.

Men like her. They turn around to look as we walk down the street. I suspect she's always had a lot of male attention. In our first hotel, she meets Ben, a San Diego firefighter, and his dad. They call her darling and invite her to sit with them at the communal breakfast area by the pool while I swim.

Later she tells me, excited, "Ben and his dad told me about a great oasis in the mountains where they grow their own organic food."

"You mean San Javier? The place I suggested we visit yesterday?"

"I thought it was just a boring old church."

"Nope," I said. "It's also a Jesuit mission, founded in 1699 by Father Piccolo. It's on the Royal Road of missions built up and down the coast of the Baja and into California. They have an altarpiece with gold leaf, transported all the way from mainland Mexico . . ."

Her eyes glaze over.

"Go get dressed," she said.

"I am dressed."

"I'll do your hair and makeup. Oh, I put your suitcase up on the rack in the closet. I know it's hard for you to lift it that high."

I am grateful. Though I thought my hair was done and why do I need makeup?

I drive the winding road up the Sierra de la Giganta to San Javier. Mountains covered with desert flora: cardon cacti, jumping cholla, regular cholla.

"I can't believe there is a desert right beside the ocean," she enthuses.

"This is part of the Sonoran Desert. It goes all the way up to Canada," I say, then realize I am channelling my dad, who liked to provide information, going so far as bringing the encyclopedia to the dinner table to answer our questions. I love the desert colours, ochre and sage, but having grown up in a desert in British Columbia, I know the dangers: the soaring temperatures that can lead to dehydration and death, the preponderance of spiny plants, cacti, rattlesnakes, scorpions. But I don't say anything to Ayuko, not wanting to scare her.

We park by the church, and she agrees to give it a quick peruse. Then we walk down the shady path behind it, beside the narrow canals with burbling water, olive trees and grape vines planted by the Jesuit fathers. She stops to identify the flowers, tells me about the succulents, for which I am grateful, being somewhat interested in plants but never really paying attention to their names. She has a beautiful garden at home, purple-and-yellow-themed flowers in lovely tangled profusion.

In the village café, she orders her usual: steamed fish and vegetables with sushi rice (she is always hopeful even though I tell her there will never be sushi rice, only yellow Mexican rice). She does sample a few totopos (fresh tortilla chips fried in local olive oil), and although she generally won't eat anything fried, pronounces them delicious.

Ayuko hasn't travelled much as an adult. She lived in Japan and then Hong Kong and China as a girl. Her parents "gave" her to her aunt and uncle to raise in China. They wanted her to see the world. Her aunt and uncle were in the gemstone business and travelled all over. "But they were always pulling me out of school when they went on business trips. I loved school and I didn't want to miss it. I hated being behind the other kids."

She immigrated to Canada with her aunt and uncle at age eight. At fourteen, when they planned to move from Calgary, she protested, said she wasn't going to leave school. They left her in the care of a guardian. She's been working ever since she was fourteen.

Because of her history, I try to be patient and understanding when she asks questions: "Why do we have to pay for the bathroom here?" ("It's someone's job."); "Why is there garbage everywhere?" ("They don't really have the infrastructure we have, garbage pick-up, city services.").

I hate clothes shopping, but Ayuko loves it. We visit most of the *tiendas* in Loreto. I pass judgement on hats ("cute/so-so"), dresses ("too big/too much material/perfect"), scarves ("bad colour on you/good colour on you").

"Why don't you try something on?" she asks.

"I don't need any more clothes," I say, my interest in shopping having waned with age.

By day five, her suitcase is bulging, and I add some of her purchases to mine: a flowered tunic, embroidered white dress, hat painted with butterflies and flowers, on which she plans to paint purple flourishes when she gets home.

BY THE TIME I THOUGHT I might have children, I was her age, thirty-eight. I've always loved kids, my speech therapy clients, my niece and nephew. My friends' kids called me Auntie. In my thirties, when I went to Cuba to study Spanish, my best friend was a four-year-old, Haley. Her parents were busy with their two other kids so I was happy to take her off their hands. Playing with children makes me happy.

Thirty-eight turned into thirty-nine, forty, forty-one. At forty-two I was in a relationship with a younger man, M, who wanted children. He cooed over babies, any child really. And I could have had them. But I was starting a new job in a different city, and he had plans in another country that included saving the workers/starting a revolution. These plans didn't include me.

I'M SITTING ON A SHADED BENCH in the Loreto *zocalo*, the central plaza, while Ayuko browses the shops. She is comfortable going in the stores without me now, having realized most shopkeepers speak some English. I watch two preschoolers with long braids chase each other up and down the bandstand stairs. A blonde girl joins in. Sweet.

A man carrying a girl sits on a nearby bench. Two women walk toward him. Hey, I know them!

"Rosita!" I call, surprised, not expecting to see her until we are back from La Paz.

The man is Rosita's son-in-law, the other woman her daughter, the girl her granddaughter, Evelina. Ayuko returns with another new hat and we all decide we need ice cream. Evie takes my hand and chatters about her dancing. Ayuko, who was a child ballerina, demonstrates ballet moves outside the store while the rest of us slurp our melting cones.

"We can babysit," I say to Rosita, "if you guys want some time together."

"Thanks, but I love to be with Evie."

AT CHRISTMAS ONE YEAR at my parents' house, M fell in love with my real four-year-old niece. She trailed after him, persuaded him to read her yet another Robert Munsch book, play hide-and-seek. He fetched her orange juice with the pulp strained out, just the way she liked it.

Now he is married with a ten-year-old daughter. I mention this to Ayuko.

"How do you know?"

"Um, I went online."

"You cyberstalked him?"

"Kind of."

"You shouldn't do that."

"I just want to know if he is all right. It's harmless."

"It is not harmless!"

She may be right. I don't just want to know he is okay. I want to have some sort of connection with him. But I know that any contact will lead to endless musing about what could have been.

"Believe me, I know. I was engaged for five years to a British guy. He was traumatized from the army, his time in the desert in Iraq," she says.

I imagine the desert in Iraq as a hell, hotter than the thirty degrees it is here.

"I know. M too, from his time in prison in his country."

"Those kinds of guys do not make good husbands," Ayuko insists. "They are not there for us. We can try and try, but we can't change them, and we end up tying ourselves in knots. Better to be alone."

Who is the aunt and who is the niece now?

WE ARE EIGHT on the seven-day kayak trip circumnavigating Espíritu Santo Island. Our companions are a fit, fiftyish

Colorado couple, a young couple touring the world on bikes, and Jorge, a young Mexican businessman. Our guide is thirty-nine-year-old Chino.

When Ayuko and I planned the trip, we agreed that I would be the brains, the speaker, the driver, the planner, and she would be the brawn. She has been hauling my suitcase on and off luggage racks and up steep stairs; now she carries my duffle bag from the boat, helps me set up my tent on the sand in the hot, shadeless afternoons.

But she is having trouble kayaking. The week before we left, she said she wanted to paddle by herself, so I changed our reservation from a double to single kayaks. The first day her feet couldn't reach the pedals to control the rudder, so she didn't use it. The second day, she got the rudder adjusted but pressed it back and forth, zigzagging from side to side. She holds the paddle tight, pulling instead of the effortless pushing that takes you farther and prevents your neck and shoulders from hurting.

"Aren't you sore from paddling?" she asks.

"Nope. I've done this a lot." Indeed, kayaking feels effortless to me. Being in or on the ocean lulls me into a peaceful, meditative state.

I try to give her advice, but she likes to "learn by myself." As she did at school, I imagine, her aunt and uncle busy with their business, leaving her to her own devices. I understand but feel disappointed. I can help her, prevent her from being in pain. But she doesn't want any help.

At happy hour on our camping beach one night, I hear her asking the men to paddle with her: Jorge declines, saying he prefers a single; Chino says he has to be in a single in case someone gets in trouble. A double is found for her, but I am not her partner.

She offers Chino a massage.

"We are not allowed to touch the clients and clients are not allowed to touch us," he says.

He then tells the group about a walk we can do independently to a pocket beach on the other side of the cove.

"Can you take me there, Chino?" Ayuko asks. He declines, saying he needs to be available to all of the clients.

"Is he married?" she asks me later.

"He told us he was, remember?" I say.

After the kayak trip, we drive in the heat to my favourite beach, Juncalito, south of Loreto.

I wade into the clear water, then dive under, savouring the refreshing shock of coolness. I do a few strokes, and my body slowly warms. Turn on my back to float under a cerulean sky. Stare at ochre hills, dotted with cordon cacti rising in the near distance; beyond them the shimmering, sage-coloured Sierra de la Giganta. I drift in beauty, cradled in my ocean by the desert.

Ayuko shows me the treasures she collected in a bucket while I was swimming: an oyster shell (she had cracked it and eaten the oyster), two small crabs, assorted other shells.

"Beautiful," I said. "I hope that oyster didn't have red tide."

"What's red tide?"

"An algae that contaminates oysters. And people."

"I'm fine."

I am about to say more and think back to the risks in my youth, riding motorcycles with guys I'd just met in Indonesia, hiking by myself in the Yunga mountains in Bolivia, riding chicken buses through the mountains of Kashmir. I thought myself invincible at her age too.

We are staying with Rosita in Nopolo outside Loreto, in a condo with good wi-fi, something we haven't had for a while. I scroll through my personal Facebook feed, then check my public author page. Someone has posted a message.

I don't read it right away, thinking I'll respond when I get home. But the poster's name niggles at me. His first name is M's nickname. I check. It is M. He asks if he can call me, says he needs my help.

"Don't answer him," says Ayuko when I tell mention it to her and Rosita. "Block him immediately."

"You have to look after yourself. He broke your heart," Rosita adds.

"But I want to help him."

"Why?" Ayuko asks.

"Because I like helping people." Liar. Well, I do. But that is not why I want to answer him.

"You can help people. Just not him," Rosita insists.

"Mm-hmm."

"You have to have boundaries. You have to respect yourself. You have to stay above the water," Ayuko adds.

She is right. I am a good swimmer. But good swimmers can get caught in currents, be spit up like so much detritus on a garbage beach. Like the one where Ayuko and I found ourselves yesterday at the end of a hot, cacti-laden dirt track. It looked pristine from the road but was strewn with plastic bags, beer bottles, and fish heads.

Ayuko loves the apartment that I've booked for our last three days in Loreto. She is determined to cook, and we visit the *supermercado*, bring back a haul of vegetables, fruit, meat and fish, and amazingly, something resembling sushi rice.

"We only have three more days," I tell her. "How can we possibly eat all this food?"

We will, she says, and we do. She concocts delicious meals: pork stir fry, shrimp tacos. She invites our hosts, Steve, a retired lawyer from Oregon, and Adriana, his Mexican wife, to eat with us. In the evenings, Steve brings out two guitars and we play some favourite songs: "Wild World," "Catch the Wind," "Me and Bobby McGee." Ayuko doesn't know the songs, but she seems to like them. I tell her about my backpacking days in Europe, when we'd have singalongs in youth hostels, someone playing the hostel's battered old guitar.

"Sounds fun," she says wistfully. "I wish I was talented like you."

"You are plenty talented. You paint, you draw, you cook, you grow gorgeous flowers."

"I guess," she says wistfully. And I think of the motherless child, on her own at fourteen. Think of her following her aunt and uncle all over China, across Canada. Being pulled out of school just as she starting to make friends, getting settled. I contemplate the guts it must have taken her to tell them that she was not going to move with them, she was going to stay in Calgary. At the age she was working as a hairdresser's apprentice, I was spending lazy summer days on the beach, swimming, tanning, chasing boys.

BACK IN CALGARY, Ayuko invites me to a Chinese noodle house. In Mandarin, she orders hand-rolled noodle soup and dumplings for us. Serves me the best pieces of meat and noodles. Like M used to do for me when he served the Persian dishes he loved: *lubia polo, keshmesh polo.* Rice dishes studded with meat and vegetables.

She invites me over to play cribbage. I decline, saying I have tickets to a concert: Martyn Joseph, a Welsh singer-songwriter I first saw at the Calgary Folk Music Festival in the late 1990s. She's never heard of him. Or the folk festival. Or folk music. I explain what it is, how it is world music, singer-songwriter music, ballads about freedom and social justice.

"That sounds a bit boring."

"It's not. You liked the music Steve and I played in Loreto. That was folk music."

"Okay, I guess I like some folk music," she laughs.

She doesn't ask if I answered M and I don't tell her that I did. That he wanted help writing a letter to the government. His wife couldn't help, her English isn't good perhaps. I was shocked he would ask after all these years. But I did it. Against my own and my friends' better judgement, I answered him.

There is a desert by the ocean. Beautiful from afar, but fiery hot and full of thorns.

SEVENTEEN POSTCARDS

1.

Bolivia, 2009

I am paging through *El Deber* (The Duty) newspaper when Richard points to a white-haired man in a wheelchair outside his teachers' workroom and says, "There's the man who caught Che Guevara."

I know that Santa Cruz de la Sierra, this eastern Bolivian city, is conservative, the heart of the opposition to Evo Morales's Socialist government. I'd assumed that the army commander who'd captured Che Guevara at La Higuera, a few hundred kilometres to the southwest, was dead.

And General Gary Prado Salmón, a man who had argued against Che's execution, is very much alive.

"What's he doing at your university?"

"Visiting friends," my Cuban friend answers. "He was a professor here."

2.

In the two days I've been visiting Richard, I have met many Cuban *profes*, including Magaly, who is married to Inti Peredo's son. Inti, a Bolivian Communist who fought with Che, lived clandestinely after Che's death, continuing the struggle to liberate the impoverished country from military rule and establish a socialist state until government soldiers captured, tortured, and executed him. The Cuban government brought his widow and children to live in Cuba. Magaly's mother-in-law still lives in Havana, where Richard's sister, Juana, visits her, bringing gifts for El Tío, the Bolivian Lord of the Underworld. He rules over the miners, offering protection if appeased, or destruction if not. El Tío presides over her living room altar.

3.

At the outdoor market, Richard steers his Toyota down a dirt track past stalls laden with fruit. The stalls are attended by women from western Bolivia, their braids and pleated skirts swinging as they approach the car.

He asks for mandarin oranges, bananas, papayas, mangos.

I take some *bolivianos* from my wallet, but Richard gives me his teacher look and says my name, the way he might say "Yes?" to an argumentative student or a statement I make about Canadian government perfidy. Though he is more likely to believe me now, having lived outside of Cuba and been exposed to the perfidies of non-Communist governments for ten years.

In 1999, I spent an afternoon in a pizza restaurant in Havana Vieja, explaining the concept of a mortgage to him.

"But if you cannot pay the mortgage, your government will give you another house so you will not be homeless."

"Nope. The government doesn't care."

"But how is it possible?"

"That's capitalism for you."

He shakes his head. "In Cuba everyone has a home. No money, maybe. But all people have a place to live."

4.

We idle at a busy Santa Cruz intersection, waiting for the light to change. Children wander through the traffic proffering gum, candy, newspapers. Stoned teenagers and old men come to car windows, begging for change.

"That is where the free Cuban clinic is," Richard says, pointing down an alley. "The government doesn't want to advertise it, because of the anti-Evo sentiment here."

After Evo Morales's party, Movimiento al Socialismo (MAS), won the election in 2009, there were right-wing demonstrations in Santa Cruz. Neo-Nazi groups harassed party supporters. Cubans received death threats.

The government is encouraging social responsibility. They have told the owners of Richard's university that it will be nationalized unless it participates in projects to educate the poor. Richard thinks this is an excellent idea. He doesn't understand some of his colleagues' reluctance to embrace Evo's plans. But then he spent his life working for socialist ideals.

While I have spent much of mine reading about them. Inspired by what I saw on an educational tour of Cuba in 1997, I read books about the 1959 revolution, Fidel, Che. I became obsessed. Some might say brainwashed. My friend Mercedes,

Richard's sister, for one. But then she left Cuba for Canada under very different circumstances.

5.

Sunday. The usual heavy Santa Cruz traffic is lighter. We are heading west to Güembé, a private water park and nature reserve outside of town. We cross the Piraí River and follow a rough road past gated mansions of the wealthy, many built with drug money, according to Richard.

"The rich want to make it hard for ordinary people to get here," he says, steering around a series of potholes.

Güembé's parking lot is full of gleaming SUVs. Richard insists on paying the twenty-dollar-U.S. entrance fee. We wander around the netted bird observatory, the parrots swooping low as if to pose for our cameras.

At the buffet restaurant, we are surrounded by large, loud family groups, their plates piled high with food. Richard points out a man at the next table. "He was a minister in the previous government. He is fighting Evo."

I wait in line for dessert, too politely it seems because people push ahead of me, giving orders to the teenager, who averts her eyes and says, "*Si, señora. Si, patrón.*" Richard told me when he first came to Santa Cruz, he was shocked at how people called him *patrón*. As if he were the master and they serfs.

6.

We are at Dumbo's restaurant, a place I remember from my last visit in 2000. The waiters wear masks against H1N1 influenza. The patrons don't.

"We were here ten years ago with a Cuban professor. I can't remember his name. Alejandro?"

Richard pinches his brown skin. "*El prieto*? The really black guy?"

I smile at the Cuban habit of calling people by a prominent feature—the fat one, the bald one, the big-nosed one.

"Yes."

"You have a good memory."

"Actually, I have a terrible memory," I counter. "I can't remember what I ate for breakfast this morning. Though from the size of that haul you got at the market, I'd guess fruit."

We talk about the Cuban movie *Fresa y chocolate*. Havana's Coppelia ice cream parlour was featured in the first scene where Diego, the gay artist, met David, the straight Communist.

"You know the things that Diego loved: the music, the art, books? Those things are the best things of Cuba. Diego represented what is good about my country. If he would not do his art, he has to leave. I mean if he could not. Which is it?"

That troublesome conditional tense.

"It depends on your meaning."

"He needed his art to live."

"Could not."

"I thought Cubans could do the impossible," I want to say to my friend who volunteered to teach in Angola, cut sugarcane in the Cuban countryside, helped build Havana's Pan-American Stadium and his own Havana apartment building, but the waiter comes with our sundaes.

Richard, still struggling with the English conditional, says: "If I had stayed in Cuba, maybe I could not be alive now."

"What do you mean?"

"If I stayed, I could not send money to help my family."

His sisters, niece, ex-wife, son.

"You mean because of the stress of not being able to help them?"

"Yes. Maybe. I must look after my family. It is *mi deber*. And also, I am a dreamer."

"Me too."

"Yes, I know. But in Cuba, a dreamer is a hard thing to be."

7.

Richard is teaching all day, so I hire a taxi to take me to a Jesuit mission in the Chiquitania area, northeast of Santa Cruz.

The people of Chiquitania were converted by the Jesuits in the seventeenth and eighteenth centuries. They left behind a series of mission churches blending European and indigenous architectural styles and painted with their intricate designs.

The missions were independent of the Spanish crown because of their remote locations. People looking for protection could join these missions, where they could own land and had time for making art. The church fathers brought musicians from Europe to teach music. Chiquitano orchestras played compositions on handmade instruments. In 1975, when restoration work was being done on one of the mission churches, six thousand baroque scores were unearthed.

My taxi lurches to a stop behind a line of cars at an army checkpoint outside a village. The driver, Ruben, points to an indigenous woman selling cheese buns, *cuñapés*, and tells me in Spanish that this area is now populated by people from western Bolivia who make trouble.

I've read that some of the people who moved to the more prosperous east were impoverished silver miners from Potosí. I don't tell Ruben I'd been to Cerro Rico, crawled down mine tunnels where I encountered El Tío, his alter covered with cigarettes, coca leaves, and glasses of alcohol, offerings from the miners to keep them safe.

"They only moved here to help elect Evo," Ruben says.

"Perhaps they came to find work."

"These people didn't come here for work. They came to vote for MAS. They blockaded the roads. They burned things down. What do you do in your country with such people?"

My Spanish is not up to explaining the idealism of the Pierre Trudeau era I grew up in. A time before the internment of Canadians of Ukrainian and Japanese descent and the horrors of residential schools became widely known. In my country they might be arrested. But I don't say this to Ruben.

8.

Richard shows me a picture of his mother, Caridad, as a young bride. I see her resemblance to the old woman I knew, the large and expressive eyes her son inherited. Before the Cuban revolution, Caridad worked as a maid. After the revolution, the government gave her a house and training, sent her children to university.

Richard left Cuba at the age of forty-two, ten years ago, ostensibly to attend a conference in Bolivia. The government let him go, believing he'd return.

"I came here with nothing," he tells me. "My university gave me a three-hundred-dollar advance. It seemed like a fortune."

"Your mother must have been sad to see you leave."

"Yes. You know, she died before I could get permission to return. I miss her every day. But I say to myself I would do, should do my best for her, to make her proud. I have to do that every day. It is—how do you say?—*mi deber*."

"Your duty."

9.

Mercedes phones her brother every day that I'm visiting him.

"Your sister calls you a lot."

"She wants to make sure I am okay and that I am looking after you properly. She likes to control me," he says.

"You don't mind?"

"Of course not. She's my sister. I love her."

He searches through his photo album. "I have a nice picture of you in the flower dress. I want to show you."

"Are you sure? I don't usually wear florals."

"*Por supuesto*. The dress was covered with roses."

Then I remember—I did have a dress my parents gave me for Christmas one year. In Cuba, I wore flowers.

10.

Richard says I have sent him seventeen postcards since we first met in 1999. Some of them are displayed around the living room of his apartment, tacked to the wall above his bookshelf. Postcards from Armenia and the Philippines where I did volunteer work, Turkey where I visited archeological sites, the Baja where I kayaked, the Grand Canyon where I hiked. All the places I was free to travel because I come from a developed country, have had the privilege of being able to go to school, work at what I want, do what I please.

11.

I'm reading in the lobby of the strangely named Hotel Alaska, where I'm staying because Richard's friend is using his apartment to make a film. Waiting for Richard to finish teaching and visit me. When he arrives, we go up to my room. I perch at the edge of the bed, Richard on the edge of a rickety chair. I tell him I've arranged to take a taxi to the airport.

"You're leaving?" he asks, surprised.

I told him yes, tomorrow morning.

"Already? I thought you should stay longer."

"*Would* stay longer. But I told you my plans."

"You did not." Teacher voice again.

"I did. I sent you an email."

"You told me in an email?"

I did. He doesn't always answer my emails. I thought it was because he was too busy. But maybe he doesn't check them obsessively the way I do. Maybe he tells people important things to their faces.

"I'm sorry. I should have mentioned it again."

He looks sad. "Okay. I don't want to stop you. You have everything planned. Do what you want."

The thing is, I *could* change my flight and stay longer. I'd planned to go next to the old gold-mining city of Ouro Preto in Brazil. I want to see this World Heritage Site, the baroque buildings that gold built. I thought five days would be enough time here. I didn't want to impose because I knew he'd insist on paying for everything. But now I want to stay.

12.

We walk through the narrow, dark streets of the downtown. Ahead of us on the broken sidewalk, an old man weaves from side to side and then out into the street. Richard speeds past me, takes the man's arm, and guides him gently to the other side.

"Drunk?" I ask.

"Blind. I've seen him fall. I've seen him smash his head into a wall."

"That's terrible. Doesn't he have a white cane?"

"He won't use it. My grandfather was blind and he was the same."

I later learn that Mario Terán, the Bolivian army sergeant who carried out the orders to shoot Che Guevara, went blind from cataracts. His sight was restored by volunteer Cuban doctors in Santa Cruz.

Both Richard and I have macular degeneration, but his vision is stronger than mine.

13.

The nine-hour bus ride from São Paulo to Ouro Preto takes fourteen. I arrive at midnight to find the station and streets deserted. I pull on a coat against the cold drizzle and wait for a taxi to drive by. At the corner, some guys in a muscle car crank the rap, drink from a communal bottle, and take turns staring at me. I question myself in the conditional: If I disappeared right now, would anyone here miss me? Would anyone even know I was gone?

14.

When I first met Richard in 1997, he claimed I almost killed him. I'd arrived in Havana for a tour with the Canada–Cuba Friendship Society, a group of lively, argumentative Communists who accepted me only after learning that my grandmother had been a party member (before Stalin).

I arranged to meet Richard to give him the presents Mercedes had sent with me. I was charmed by his intelligence, sense of humour, and lovely manners. I invited him to go bike riding, and we rode to Hemingway's farm, Finca Vigía, eighty kilometres away. It was a hot day and there were a lot of hills. He didn't complain. I learned later he had rarely ridden a bike. That he had trouble walking for days afterwards.

15.

The narrow-gauge train from Ouro Preto to Mariana winds slowly up the side of a steep mountain canyon, past villages and abandoned gold mines. Children stand inches from the tracks, hands out, waiting for coins.

Mariana is town of baroque churches. One, the Catedral Basílica da Sé, is hosting an organ recital. It's an hour-long concert, and I have two hours to wait until the train returns to Ouro Preto, so I sit down in a back pew. The organist plays a series of baroque pieces. Then she begins a simple piece, in a haunting minor key. I look at my program. It is *Folias*, an eighteenth-century piece from the Bolivian Chiquitos.

Rain streaks the windows of the Deguste restaurant in Ouro Preto. I pick at my chicken and listen to a live Bee Gees request show on the restaurant's sound system. To request a song, you can call 1-866-beegees. Donna from Boulder asks

Robin to play "Massachusetts" and "I Started a Joke." Maria from Mexico wants to hear "Jive Talkin'" and "How Can You Mend a Broken Heart?"

16.

Mercedes told me she was grateful to come to Canada. Her husband, Ariel, a Cuban naval engineer, jumped ship in Spain and sought asylum there. Back in Havana, Mercedes was fired from her job. She was followed, her every movement monitored. She waited for Ariel to move to Canada, to establish himself, to raise the money to send for her. In the middle of one night there was a knock on the door, an official who told her she and her young son were leaving for Calgary. She wasn't allowed to say goodbye to her family. She didn't see her mother again.

Mercedes recently gave a speech about Che Guevara to her Toastmasters club. "He wasn't a saint," she told them. "He was in charge of executions after the revolution. He killed a lot of people."

17.

Che's daughter from his second marriage, Aleida, is a pediatrician and children's rights advocate. She and her siblings still live in Cuba. Aleida has worked on medical missions in Angola, Ecuador, and Nicaragua and runs homes for disabled and refugee children.

When Aleida was a girl, Che left Cuba to start revolutions abroad. He came back in disguise to visit his children, introducing himself as a friend of their father. He couldn't tell his children who he was, lest one of them divulge his whereabouts.

But young Aleida knew this stranger was someone special. She loved the stranger.

And she thought the stranger loved her.

Earlier versions of following chapters were previously published in different formats:

"The Art Hospital," in *Waiting: An Anthology of Essays*, edited by Rona Altrows and Julie Sedivy, University of Alberta Press, 2018.

"Back to the Garden," in *You Look Good for Your Age: An Anthology*, edited by R. Altrows, University of Alberta Press, 2021.

"Eggplant with Pomegranate," *The New Quarterly*, no. 122 (Spring 2012).

"Leaving Lares," *Prism International* 49, no. 3 (Spring 2011).

"Member of a Wedding," *Hippocampus* (Fall/Winter 1990).

"On Shyness and Stuttering," in *Shy: An Anthology*, edited by Naomi K. Lewis and Rona Altrows, University of Alberta Press, 2013.

"A Tale of Two Tents" (published as "The Alchemist"), *The Malahat Review*, no. 167 (Summer 2009); in *This Place a Stranger: Canadian Women Travelling Alone*, edited by Vici Johnstone, Caitlin Press, 2015; and in *Walk Myself Home: An Anthology to End Violence Against Women*, edited by Andrea Routley, Caitlin Press, 2010.

ACKNOWLEDGEMENTS

THANK YOU, first and foremost, to my beautiful family: Jocelyn, Rachel, Steve and Carson Lyman; Melissa Haynes and Steve Mahovlic; Leslie Haynes; my mom, Jessie Haynes, and papa, Sterling, who is always with us. Love you forever. And to Karin Herrero, you are *siempre en mi corazón*.

To my Cuban family: Richard, Mercedes, Juana, and Aida, for your loyal and abiding friendship.

To Hasmik and my Armenian family and Annie and my Filipino families for your kindness and support.

To Roberta Rees, Joan Crate, J. Jill Robinson, Cassy Welburn, JoAnn McCaig, Laurel Sproule, Leslie Haynes, Judy Millar, Merilyn Simonds, Rona Altrows, and Katherine Koller for your astute feedback on these essays. Special thanks to Margaret Macpherson, who read them all, asked, "Did you know you write a lot about food?" and suggested the title!

To friends Lynn Podgurny, Barry Whitehead, Sheila MacDonald, and Ayuko Yoshida for sharing these journeys with me.

To Rosita Álvarez for the Spanish and the *alma, vida,* and *sombrero*.

To Randy Earle and to my clients for your courage.

To the doctors and nurses who saved my life!

To Kim Lu at Karuna Yoga for keeping me limber.

To Susan Musgrave for the thoughtful editing and Liz Philips and the gang at Thistledown Press for bringing this book to light.

To those I met on the road.

Namaste.

ELIZABETH J. HAYNES is a retired speech-language pathologist, a traveller, and writer. Her writing has appeared in numerous magazines and anthologies, most recently *You Look Good for Your Age* (University of Alberta Press). Her short fiction collection, *Speak Mandarin not Dialect* (Thistledown Press), was an Alberta Book Award finalist. She has won the Jon Whyte Memorial Essay Award, a Western Magazine Award, and the American Heart Award for fiction. Her first novel, *The Errant Husband,* was published in 2021 (Radiant Press).